Snapping Turtle
Pet Owner's Guide.

The Captive Care of Snapping Turtles.

Including Snapping Turtles Biology, Behavior and Ecology.

by

Ben Team

ALL RIGHTS RESERVED. This book contains material protected under International and Federal Copyright Laws and Treaties.

Any unauthorized reprint or use of this material is strictly prohibited. No part of this book may be reproduced or transmitted in any form or by any means, electronic, mechanical or otherwise, including photocopying or recording, or by any information storage and retrieval system without express written permission from the author.

Copyrighted © 2015

Published by: IMB Publishing

Table of Contents

Table of Contents 3

About the Author 7

Foreword 8

Chapter 1: Snapping Turtle Description and Anatomy 16

    Basic Morphology 16

    Color and Pattern 16

    Size 17

    Shell 17

    Legs 19

    Head, Neck and Face 20

    Tail 22

    Internal Anatomy 22

Chapter 2: Snapping Turtle Biology and Behavior 26

    Growth 26

    Shedding 27

    Lifespan 28

    Senses and Intelligence 29

    Metabolism and Digestion 29

    Locomotion 29

    Diel Behavioral Patterns 30

    Seasonal Behavioral Patterns 30

    Defensive Strategies 31

    Foraging 32

    Breeding Behavior 32

Chapter 3: Snapping Turtle Taxonomy and Phylogeny 34

    Reptiles in the Tree of Life 34

Testudines in the Tree of Life 35

Snapping Turtles in the Tree of Life 36

Chapter 4: The Environment of Snapping Turtles 39

Basic Geography 39

Ecology 39

Chapter 5: Snapping Turtles as Pets: Captive Considerations 43

Snapping Turtle Suitability 43

What You'll Need 44

Costs of Captivity 45

Understanding the Commitment 46

Myths and Misunderstandings 46

Chapter 6: Snapping Turtle Husbandry 48

The Enclosure 48

Substrate and Furniture 55

Enclosure Climate 58

Lighting 67

Diet 69

Water Quality 73

Monitoring and Maintenance 76

Chapter 7: Acquiring a Snapping Turtle 80

Selecting Your Turtle 82

Chapter 8: Interacting with Your Snapping Turtle 84

Handling Snapping Turtles 84

Transporting Snapping Turtles 87

In The Event of a Bite 88

Hygiene 89

Chapter 9: Snapping Turtle Health 90

Finding a Suitable Vet 90

When to See the Vet 91

Common Health Problems 92

Quarantine 96

Chapter 10: Breeding 98

Pre-Breeding Considerations 98

Legal Issues 99

Sexing Snapping Turtles 99

Pre-Breeding Conditioning 100

Cycling 100

Pairing 102

Gravid 104

Egg Deposition 105

Egg Incubation 107

Egg Boxes 108

Incubation Media 109

The Incubator 110

Incubation Temperature and Duration 113

Sex Determination 114

Neonatal Husbandry 115

Chapter 11: Unusual Snapping Turtles 117

Common Mutations 118

Patterns of Inheritance 121

Genetic Traits and Marketing 122

Chapter 12: Supplemental Information 124

Further Reading 124

Magazines 125

Websites 125

Journals 127

Supplies 128

Support Organizations 129

Index 130

References..131

About the Author

Ben Team is an environmental educator and author with over 16 years of professional reptile-keeping experience.

Ben currently maintains www.FootstepsInTheForest.com, where he shares information, narration and observations of the natural world. When not writing about plants, animals and habitats, Ben enjoys spending time with his beautiful wife.

Foreword

Few things capture the imagination and quicken the pulse as much as the notion of prehistoric beasts lurking invisibly under the stained green surface of a murky pond.

Once bestowed with a frightening name and reputation for a vicious temperament, these leviathans rise to nearly mythological levels.

However, snapping turtles (*Chelydra serpentina* spp.) are not the product of myths and legends; they are living, breathing reptiles with whom we share our world.

In fact, those who spend time in the company of snapping turtles invariably find that -- while they command respect – snapping turtles harbor no inherent ill will toward humans.

While they feel vulnerable on dry ground and do not hesitate to mount a vigorous defense, they prefer to avoid confrontation when under water, content to spend their time hunting frogs and fish in peace.

And so they live -- quietly inhabiting waters throughout much of the Americas, playing important roles in local ecosystems. In fact, they have been doing just that for far longer than they have enthralled humans.

***

Snapping turtles have been familiar to humans for as long as humans have roamed the Americas. Native Americans prized the turtles as a food source, and they used snapping turtle shells to make ceremonial rattles and other items.

Impressed with the size of the turtles, early European settlers continued to hunt and trap the turtles for sustenance. The settlers primarily incorporated them into stews and soups, but hungry hunters and trappers also roasted fresh turtle flesh.

Snapping turtles certainly make a good food source from the human point of view, but the environment strongly disagrees with the practice.

***

In a pre-human world, adult snapping turtles feared few threats. By contrast, a wide variety of terrestrial and aquatic predators consume young snapping turtles (and the eggs from which they emerged). At best, a handful of young from each clutch manage to survive to adulthood.

Nevertheless, this system worked well for snapping turtles, because the adults did not die very often. Newly matured turtles or those who wandered in from other water bodies replaced those few adults that died, and these populations remained relatively stable.

However, as humans began to capture large numbers of snapping turtles, their populations began to plummet. The number of new snapping turtles entering the breeding pool was insufficient to replace those that had disappeared from it.

***

Of course, snapping turtles were not the only turtles targeted by hunters and trappers. Plenty of other species living in the same habitats, such as painted turtles (*Chrysemys picta*), chicken turtles (*Deirochelys reticularia*) and the snapping turtle's larger cousins, the alligator snapping turtles (*Macrochelys temminckii*); also found themselves on the dinner table.

However, the snapping turtle's life history was and is uniquely vulnerable to this level of predation. Snapping turtle populations dwindled, and humans did very little to stop the trend. Snapping turtles continued to be harvested for food, and few people were inclined to change the status quo.

***

The fact that snapping turtles are often portrayed as evil beasts has not helped their chances of attaining legal protection, nor has the fact that they continue to be (mistakenly) blamed for reductions in gamefish and waterfowl populations.

Of course, neither of these contentions is true. Snapping turtles are quite shy when encountered in the water; it is only when they are confronted on dry ground that they display irritable temperaments. Even in such cases, the turtles would rather avoid contact with humans than engage in conflict with a creature many times their size.

Their reputation with sportsmen and sportswomen is similarly undeserved. The impact snapping turtles have on gamefish and waterfowl populations is negligible at worst. In fact, it is quite likely that snapping turtle populations help improve gamefish populations, by feeding on non-game species that compete with bass, bluegill and catfish.

Game wardens and researchers have understood this for decades, yet the general populace has yet to accept this fact and change their attitudes toward these amazing animals.

Cursed by a terrible public perception – which is exacerbated by the discomfort the general population often feels about reptiles – has caused few states to offer snapping turtles any type of legal protection. It remains legal to trap snapping turtles in many parts of their range, and some states allow essentially unlimited harvests of the species.

Accordingly, people continue to decimate wild snapping turtle populations at an alarming rate. Some researchers fear that the fate of snapping turtles has already been sealed in some parts of their range, as too many adults have been removed from the breeding pool to allow a recovery.

***

Given the impressive nature of snapping turtles, it should come as no surprise that many people have begun to keep them as pets. While snapping turtles present several challenges, they do make excellent pets in the proper circumstances.

In most cases, the difference between success and failure with the species hinges on the keeper's experience level, dedication and willingness to continue learning about the species.

Snapping turtles are not suitable for beginners. They are challenging pets compared to beginner-friendly reptiles, such as leopard geckos (*Eublepharis macularius*), ball pythons (*Python regius*) and crested geckos (*Rhacodactylus ciliatus*), and they require an aquatic habitat. Providing an aquatic habitat increases the complexity level of the enclosure significantly. Keepers must consider factors such as water quality and temperature, in addition to the factors involved in keeping terrestrial reptiles.

The combination of the snapping turtle's temperament and large size also makes it an inappropriate species for beginners. A bite from even a relatively small snapping turtle can cause serious injury; a bite from a large one may change your life permanently.

While it is true that snapping turtles are less aggressive than is commonly supposed, and are only likely to strike out if cornered or touched, captive maintenance often *requires* the keeper to corner or touch the turtle. No one is at greater risk of a snapping turtle bite than a person with a pet snapping turtle is.

Nevertheless, keepers with several years of turtle-keeping experience can often learn to handle these animals safely, thanks to the innumerable lessons learned with other species. However, this is not a guarantee, and any who choose to keep snapping turtles should have concrete safety plans in place, should an injury occur.

When injuries like this happen, they often draw considerable attention from the media, which reflects poorly on the reptile hobby as a whole. Accordingly, snapping turtle keepers are not only accountable to themselves, but to the entire hobby as well.

Do not forget that you will also need to prevent unauthorized fingers and paws from accessing a snapping turtle's enclosure; as such trespasses can have horrific results.

***

Unfortunately, a large number of beginning reptile keepers lose interest in their pet after a short time. In a best-case scenario, the owner finds a suitable new home for their pet after searching for weeks or months; in a worst-case scenario, the owner fails to find a new owner, gives up and neglects the pet, who then dies a long, slow death.

While not an infallible solution, restricting snapping turtle ownership to experienced keepers helps to avoid this problem.

Experienced keepers better understand the nature and demands of long-term reptile husbandry than new keepers do. While the same could be said of those seeking to keep any long-lived reptile, long-term commitment is especially important when considering snapping turtles, as few avenues allow you to exit the endeavor.

While you may find adoptive parents for your pet leopard gecko (an 8-inch-long lizard that lives about a decade or so); you will not find many people looking for a 14-inch turtle with a bad attitude and a lifespan measured in decades.

Contrary to popular belief, your local zoo does not want your snapping turtle, nor does the local pet store. Releasing long-term pets back into the wild can cause a litany of problems and is highly discouraged. In fact, the release of unwanted pets is a criminal offense in many places. In all places, it is a threat to wild populations, as your pet may introduce foreign parasites or disease – even if snapping turtles are native to your area.

Even if you find someone to take your turtle, you will still bear the responsibility of ensuring the owner to be is qualified to keep the animal. You may even find be held liable if the new owner suffers an injury.

Despite these challenges, those who elect to keep a snapping turtle as a pet are often rewarded with the chance to spend decades in the company of one of the world's most fascinating animals.

***

As you read this book and ponder the ways in which you will care for your pet snapping turtle, remember that reptile husbandry is a much younger discipline than mammal or bird husbandry is.

Humans have been breeding and keeping mammals and birds for thousands of years, but reptile keeping has only been a mainstream pursuit for a few decades at best (although zoo keepers and scientists have been keeping reptiles in captivity for longer than that).

Even the world's leading keepers continue to learn more about the animals they keep and explore new husbandry paradigms. Provided that you pay attention to your animals and endeavor to improve your skills, you will do the same.

Although reptile husbandry continues to progress as a discipline, and many of the basic tenants have almost universal support, keepers often exhibit differing approaches.

Some of these differing approaches stem from the fact that humans are individuals, likely to approach challenges in different ways. This is as natural as it is in any other endeavor, and it contributes to innovation.

Varying value systems also influence these differences. For example, some keepers value the aesthetic value of their reptile enclosures, while others place a premium on functionality and ease of maintenance.

Cutting edge strategies and creative solutions to problems are often met with a mixture of support and disapproval.

But even mundane husbandry parameters, such as feeding frequency and basking temperatures, cause disagreements.

Given this, the best approach for most keepers is to examine the strategies used by others, and experiment with different husbandry protocols until finding the best one.

Accordingly, you will find that this book rarely identifies a given solution to a husbandry problem as the "best" or "worst." Instead, this book strives to examine a variety of such solutions, and provide the reader with some of the most important benefits and drawbacks to each approach.

Ultimately, you are responsible for your snapping turtle's well-being. The best way to provide it with a high-quality life is by learning as much as you can about the species and how other keepers are maintaining them.

Chapter 1: Snapping Turtle Description and Anatomy

When you set out to care for any animal, you must begin the process by learning as much as you can about the species.

While you must eventually learn about the biology and ecology of snapping turtles (*Chelydra serpentina* spp.), begin by learning about the morphology and anatomy of these incredible creatures.

Basic Morphology

Although keepers, scientists and writers often describe snapping turtles as having a "prehistoric" appearance, snapping turtles have the same basic body plan that most other freshwater turtles do.

Their shell is the most distinctive characteristic of their bodies, but they also possess four strong legs, which allow the turtles to power themselves through both aquatic and terrestrial habitats. A long tail helps to provide stability and enhance their ability to steer through the water, while their characteristically long necks help them to capture food and defend themselves.

Color and Pattern

Snapping turtles come in a variety of colors. Some have brown, gray or olive skin, while others are nearly black. Usually, the shell is as dark as or darker than the predominant skin color.

Captive snapping turtles often have lighter colored shells and skin than wild turtles do. Dietary items can influence the color of these turtles, as can the substrate on which they live. For example, some zoos feed their turtles food that enhances the shell's red hues.

Juveniles are usually quite dark in color, and many are almost uniformly black.

Size

Snapping turtles are the largest freshwater turtle in most portions of their range; in fact, snapping turtles are among the largest freshwater turtles in the world.

Most adults reach carapace lengths of about 12 inches (30 centimeters) and weigh between 20 and 30 pounds (9 to 13 kilograms). However, large specimens may have carapaces of 18 inches (45 centimeters) and weights in excess of 75 pounds (34 kilograms).

Hatchlings begin life as relatively small turtles, with carapace lengths of about 1 to 1.25 inches (2.5 to 3 centimeters). Hatchlings weigh about one-fifth to one-quarter of an ounce (6 to 10 grams).

Shell

Like those of all other living turtles, snapping turtle shells have a top (called the carapace), a bottom (called the plastron) and a portion of the shell that connects the two on the right and left sides, called lateral bridges.

The shells are derived from a combination of the rib cage and dermal plates (bony plates that originate within the skin). On top of the bone lie keratinized plates, called scutes.

Interestingly, the plate-like bones outnumber the keratin-based scutes. This means that the margins of the scutes do not occur in the same places that the bones fuse together. This is thought to be an adaptation that makes the shell stronger.

Snapping turtles have five vertebral scutes that form a row down the center of the back. Flanking the vertebral scutes are the coastal scutes, numbering eight in total (four on each side). Around the margin of the carapace lie 22 marginal scutes, and a single nuchal scute, which sits right behind the turtle's head.

As you can see in this photo of a snapping turtle swimming near the surface, the plastron is quite small.

l. The plastron features four pairs of scutes along the midline, a single scute near the neck and three scutes on each side of the bridge.

The carapace of snapping turtles is large, robust and adorned with sharp projections along the rear margin. The plastron, however, is greatly reduced in snapping turtles. Accordingly, it offers less protection than most other turtle plastrons do.

However, the reduction in shell size allows snapping turtles much greater range of motion than other turtles have. This allows turtles to walk with their bodies held high off the ground, and move more nimbly than many other species can.

Upon hatching, snapping turtles have three rows of keels along their carapaces. However, these keels become less conspicuous with age – many mature snapping turtles have essentially smooth carapaces.

Turtles are firmly attached to their shells; they cannot crawl out of them, as is frequently seen in cartoons and comic strips. Accordingly, a turtle's shell grows along with the turtle.

The periodic nature of this phenomenon (the shells grow quickly during the active season and cease growing in the winter) causes growth rings to form on the scutes. However, contrary to popular perception, studies have shown that the growth rings are not a reliable indicator of an individual's age.

In some cases, turtles produce more than one growth ring per year; other turtles live in areas with very long growing seasons and short (or absent) dormant seasons, which disrupts the annual nature of the process. Additionally, the shells of many turtles – particularly mature specimens – show signs of wear. If this wear occurs near the growth rings, some of the rings may be obscured.

Legs
Snapping turtles have four strong legs, which are covered in thick skin and armor-like scales. Their feet are partially webbed, although long, thick claws extend beyond the

margin of the webbing. Snapping turtles bear five toes on their front feet and four toes on their rear feet.

While their feet allow them to swim very well, they are well adapted to terrestrial locomotion, and snapping turtles are capable of walking long distances across dry ground. In addition to locomotion, snapping turtles use their legs to manipulate food items, defend themselves and dig nests.

Snapping turtles have very strong, thick claws that they use when digging or defending themselves.

Head, Neck and Face

Snapping turtles have relatively large, triangular heads, which sit at the end of their impressively long necks. Their necks are about the same length as their carapaces are. This gives snapping turtles a relatively large radius in which they can capture food or bite threats.

Snapping turtles cannot draw their head into their shells. However, they have thick, bony heads, which probably arose in conjunction with the reduction of their shells.

Like all other living turtles, snapping turtles lack teeth. Instead, they have a bony beak (technically called a rhamphotheca), which is covered by a layer of keratin.

Their beaks have evolved a sharp, cutting edge that helps them slice food into smaller pieces. The front of their beak ends in a point, which helps to ensure captured prey does not escape.

Snapping turtle eyes sit on the dorsal surface of the head, which allows them to see in front of their face, to the sides and above their heads. Snapping turtles have two nostrils that project very slightly from the face. Like most other aquatic turtles, snapping turtles lack external ears, but they do possess internal ears.

Numerous tubercles or other fleshy projections adorn the heads and necks of snapping turtles. These structures may serve as a form of camouflage or they may provide more surface area. This increased surface area improves the species' ability to absorb dissolved oxygen from the water.

The long necks of snapping turtles allow them to reach the surface to breathe more easily.

Tail

Snapping turtles have very long tails – it is one of their most distinctive features. When seen walking on land, the tail drags behind them on the ground.

Snapping turtles have three rows of keels along their tails.

Internal Anatomy

While the average turtle keeper need not understand the internal anatomy of their pet enough to perform exploratory surgery, a basic understanding of the turtle's internal world is necessary.

In most respects, turtles have internal anatomy that is similar to that of other vertebrates, such as humans. Accordingly, special attention is warranted for those aspects that differ from those of most other animals.

Skeletal System

One of the most unique aspects of the internal anatomy of snapping turtles is their skeletal system.

As with most other vertebrates, turtles have both axial and appendicular skeletons. The skull, vertebral column and ribs form the axial skeleton, while the shoulder girdle, pelvic girdle and limbs comprise the appendicular skeleton.

However, in turtles, the ribs are fused to the shell, which is comprised of dermal bones. Dermal bones originate from within the skin tissue.

Because the ribs are bonded to the shell, and the shell is inflexible, turtles cannot breathe in the same manner that most other vertebrates do.

Unlike other vertebrates, whose pelvic and hip girdles are located outside the rib cage, snapping turtles (and other cryptodires) carry these bones inside their rib cage. While this helps to protect these areas from damage, this arrangement limits the mobility of most turtles. However, thanks to the reduction of their shells, snapping turtles remain very mobile.

Digestive System

The digestive system of snapping turtles is similar to that of other turtles, and, to a lesser extent, vertebrates in general.

Just inside the mouth likes the esophagus, which transports food to the stomach. From here, food passes through the small and then large intestines before being expelled from the vent.

The pancreas and spleen lie close to the stomach, while the gallbladder attaches to the liver, just as it does in most other vertebrates.

Circulatory and Pulmonary System

In general, the circulatory and pulmonary systems of turtles are similar to those of other reptiles.

Turtles inhale through the mouth or nose, thereby allowing the air to pass through the trachea and into the two lungs. Because the turtle's shell is rigid, which prevents the ribs from moving (which would pump air into and out of the lungs), turtles have a collection of membranes and connective tissues that attach to the distal ends of the lungs. When these connective tissues contract and relax, the lungs empty and fill with air.

Like many other reptiles, turtles have three-chambered hearts, which feature two atria and a single ventricle. One atria accepts oxygenated blood from the lungs, while the other atrium receives oxygen-poor blood from the body.

Both atria pump blood into a single ventricle, which then pumps the blood into the rest of the body. Normally, as in many other reptiles, this means that the turtle's body receives a combination of oxygen-rich and oxygen-poor blood. However, turtles have a primitive septum (wall) in their ventricle, which partially prevents the mixing of the two types of blood.

Accordingly, turtles have a slightly more efficient cardiovascular system than lizards and snakes.

It is important to understand that, as with many other turtles, snapping turtles are capable of absorbing oxygen while underwater via highly vascularized tissues in the throat and cloaca.

When oxygen is absorbed via these pathways, the oxygen passes directly into the bloodstream.

Urinary System
Snapping turtles filter waste products from their bloodstream via their paired kidneys. They then release the waste products, which are primarily composed of urea and ammonia, although some uric acid may be released as well.

Turtles have a renal portal blood system, which means that the blood traveling through the rear half of the turtles' body is filtered by the kidneys before making it to the front half of the body. This has important implications in turtle medical care; medications cannot be injected into the rear half of the body, as they kidneys will filter the medications before they can circulate widely.

Reproductive System
Turtles engage in internal fertilization, so they must mate to reproduce.

Males have a single intromittent organ (penis), making them similar to crocodilians and birds, but very different from snakes and lizards, who possess paired reproductive organs (termed hemipenes).

The penis of male snapping turtles is held inverted, inside the tail base. During mating attempts, the penis everts and protrudes outside of the vent.

Females have a pair of ovaries, in which eggs form and reside; and a pair of oviducts, which accept the eggs once they are released. The eggs join the sperm inside the oviducts, where they develop.

Before the eggs are deposited, calcium and other minerals coat the surface of the developing embryos, thus giving rise to the shell.

Female snapping turtles can retain sperm from a single mating for multiple years. This is likely an adaptation that allows females to disperse widely and continue to reproduce, even if breeding partners cannot be found in new water bodies.

Chapter 2: Snapping Turtle Biology and Behavior

Now that you are familiar with the basic body plan and morphology of snapping turtles, you should learn about their biology and behavior. In other words, after having learned what snapping turtles *are*, you must learn what they *do*.

Growth

Snapping turtles are relatively quick-growing turtles while young, but their growth rate slows considerably once they reach maturity. Some turtles may cease growing completely upon reaching maturity, but most continue to add length and mass, albeit at a very slow rate.

The growth rate of snapping turtles varies significantly in relation to the amount of food they can acquire and the climate in which they live (longer growing seasons allow the turtles to consume more food in a given year). Captive snapping turtles usually grow more quickly than wild specimens do.

Snapping turtles hatch from their eggs measuring about 1 to 1.25 inches (2 to 3 centimeters) in carapace length. By the time they have reached one year of age, wild snapping turtles usually reach about 3 to 5 inches (7.6 centimeters to 12.7 centimeters) in length. Thanks to their essentially infinite food supply, captive-raised snapping turtles may exceed these growth rates.

By the end of their second year, captive snapping turtles (or those living in warm, productive ponds) are approaching 6 inches (15 centimeters) in carapace length. After this time, their growth begins to slow. Most individuals reach about 10 inches (25 centimeters) by 5 to 10 years of age, although well-fed captives may exceed this growth rate considerably.

After reaching about 10 inches in length, which is approximately the size at which they mature, snapping turtles stop growing so rapidly. Although some individuals that live in productive habitats are able to keep growing and eventually reach lengths in excess of 16 inches (40 centimeters), others are unable to acquire enough food to grow appreciably.

This means that size is a poor predictor of the age of mature turtles.

Snapping turtles typically reach weights of about 10 to 20 pounds (4.5 to 9 kilograms). However, large individuals often weigh 30 to 40 pounds (13 to 18 kilograms). Published maximum weights vary greatly, but several credible reports of 50-pound (22-kilogram) snapping turtles exist.

Shedding

Like most other reptiles, snapping turtles shed their skin; however, unlike snakes and lizards, who shed all of their scales at the same time, snapping turtles shed on a rather continual basis. This often prevents their owners from noticing the process, causing them to assume incorrectly that snapping turtles do not shed.

However, at some times – particularly during periods of rapid growth – snapping turtles may increase the amount of skin they shed in a short time period. This will cause your turtle to look as though his legs and neck are covered in a translucent film, which may tear free into long filaments. Some snapping turtles consume their shed skin, as they are able to pull it free.

Occasionally, snapping turtles may shed their scutes, but keepers rarely observe this as they do with other aquatic turtle species, such as sliders (*Trachemys scripta* spp.) or painted turtles (*Chrysemys picta*).

Scute shedding is likely more common among juveniles than it is among adults, who (at least among wild snapping turtles) often bear a thick coat of algae on their scutes. If the turtles shed often at all, these algal mats would not form.

Lifespan

Most turtles live long lives, and snapping turtles are no exception. Most mortality occurs before snapping turtles reach 3-inches (7.6 centimeters) in length; once they reach this size, they have very few natural predators. By the time they are 10 inches (25.4 centimeters) or more in length, their only significant predators are humans.

Research on snapping turtles has revealed that, in many populations, adult mortality is less than three percent annually. In some areas, less than one percent of the adults die in any given year. This mortality largely occurs due to old age, and it often occurs during the winter, when the turtles are hibernating.

The reported average lifespan for snapping turtles varies from one authority to the next. Most wild-living turtles live for at least 15 years, and many live to be 30 years of age or older. The maximum-recorded lifespan of a captive snapping turtle is 47 years, but this is unlikely to represent a very advanced age for the species. Some authorities speculate that some of the oldest, largest snapping turtles exceed 100 years of age.

Senses and Intelligence

Snapping turtles possess the same senses that most other turtles do. They have reasonably good eyesight, respond to tactile stimulation readily and appear to have a strong sense of smell. Some experts believe that snapping turtles hear well, while others believe that their sense of hearing is average (relative to other turtles, which are generally thought to have poor hearing) at best.

Turtles have a larger brain size index than most lizards and snakes, but this does not mean they are especially intelligent. Nevertheless, snapping turtles do exhibit some problem solving abilities and learn to anticipate husbandry protocols and feeding times.

Metabolism and Digestion

Snapping turtles – like most other non-avian reptiles – have slow metabolisms. According to some studies, wild snapping turtles eat about their body weight in food each year, however this likely varies from location to location. Captive turtles almost invariably consume more food than this on a yearly basis.

Interestingly, studies have shown that snapping turtles do not move to warmer microhabitats after feeding.

Locomotion

Snapping turtles do most of their underwater traveling by walking along the bottom. However, they are capable swimmers, who use their webbed feet to propel themselves through the water with ease. While snapping turtles are not as graceful in the water as slider turtles or softshell turtles (*Apalone* spp.), they swim well enough to meet their needs.

They are often seen swimming to the water's surface, where they will suspend and bask in the morning sunlight.

Snapping turtles are also capable of walking on dry land. In fact, some snapping turtles have been recorded traveling more than one mile (1.6 kilometers) to reach an egg deposition site or a new body of water.

Despite their bulky build and ungainly appearance, snapping turtles are actually accomplished climbers. They are routinely observed scaling downed trees, rocks and even chain-link fences.

Diel Behavioral Patterns

In general, snapping turtles are best adapted for activity during periods of low light, such as dawn and dusk. However, snapping turtles may be active at any time during the day or night.

Many, especially those living in cool climates, become active when the sun rises. By contrast, those living in warm climates may be active exclusive at night. Captive snapping turtles may be active at any time.

Seasonal Behavioral Patterns

Snapping turtles are active from early spring until the late fall in most portions of their range; however, those in southern North America, as well as Central and South America remain active year round. However, even those living in warm areas will become dormant during temporary cold snaps.

In general, snapping turtles are remarkably tolerant of low temperatures. Many individuals have been spotted swimming below frozen ponds. Occasionally, active individuals are spotted in the northern United States as early as February or as late as November.

Most mating takes place in the spring and early summer. Egg deposition occurs a few months later, with youngsters hatching in the late summer or early fall. Hatchling in northern areas may attempt to overwinter in the nest, and emerge the following spring. However, some studies have found low survival rates among hatchlings that do so.

Defensive Strategies

Hatchling and juvenile snapping turtles are vulnerable to a wide variety of predators in their natural habitats. They usually try to remain hidden (or at least inconspicuous) to avoid attracting the attention of predators. When inactive, they will bury themselves in mud, lie amid dense vegetation or crawl into tight crevices.

If they are discovered, they will try to shield themselves with their shell or swim away if encountered underwater. They may attempt to bite or scratch at the offender, but this is rarely effective enough to dissuade a hungry predator.

Adult snapping turtles fear relatively few predators. In the water, they are usually able to protect themselves by a combination of their large size, cryptic coloration and tendency to hide in inaccessible locations when inactive.

Snapping turtles usually swim away from humans when they are underwater. They only become aggressive when cornered on dry land.

On land, snapping turtles respond to threats with extreme aggression. They may snap with their jaws (the behavior that led to their common name) as well as claw with their feet. They may even defecate, presumably to make themselves less appetizing.

A large snapping turtle in a defensive posture.

Foraging

Snapping turtles actively forage for some of their food, but they also sit and wait in ambush. Both techniques prove successful, and different populations may engage in differing amounts of one strategy or the other.

Nevertheless, adults are considerably less likely to forage for food than young snapping turtles are. Young snapping turtles acquire almost all of their food by foraging.

Breeding Behavior

Shortly after emerging from hibernation, males and females begin preparing to mate. While most mating activity takes place in the spring, individuals living in warm climates may mate all throughout the active season.

Male snapping turtles usually defend their territories from other males, but they usually allow females to pass through so that they may attempt to mate with them. However, mating among snapping turtles is rarely a gentle affair, and the males often bite the females until they submit.

During mating, males will ride atop the back of the female's carapace, using their claws to hold on. Once the female has been moved into position, male turtles evert their penis, and insert them into the female's cloaca.

After successful mating, the eggs will begin to develop inside the female's body. Nesting usually begins in the early summer, but it may occur later for populations in cool regions.

When the females are ready to deposit their eggs, they leave the water and begin excavating a patch of soil near the water. After depositing their eggs, the female covers the nest and returns to the water; she will have no further contact with the young.

Some females produce a clutch in successive seasons, but many females only produce a clutch every second or third season.

Chapter 3: Snapping Turtle Taxonomy and Phylogeny

Snapping turtles are quite distinctive turtles that have been recognized as a species since Linnaeus first described them in 1758.

However, scientists have shifted their location in the tree of life several times, as new data upended previous frameworks. Similarly, the degree to which scientists acknowledge different species and subspecies of snapping turtles has changed over time.

Reptiles in the Tree of Life

For decades, scientists have debated the definition of the term "reptile." (Anderson, 2003)

On the one hand, lizards, snakes, crocodiles and turtles are all instantly recognizable as reptiles, thanks to their scaly skin and other traits.

However, the reptile evolutionary lineage, when considered in its entirety, must also include dinosaurs, and their direct descendants, the birds.

Regardless of which definition taxonomists ultimately agree upon, the history of the group is relatively well known. Reptiles first evolved approximately 300 million years ago, when they broke off the amphibian family tree.

This lineage produced an amazing array of species, including dinosaurs, mosasaurs and pterodactyls, as well as the ancestors to modern snakes, lizards and turtles. Most of these lineages died out almost completely, but a few managed to survive to the present day. Currently, reptiles are represented by the following groups:

- Crocodilians
- Squamates (snakes and lizards)
- Sphenodontids (tuataras)
- Testudines (turtles)
- Birds

Testudines in the Tree of Life

All living turtles can trace their origin back to the same ancestral species, meaning that all living turtles are part of the same evolutionary lineage. Scientists call such groups monophyletic.

Two different names are commonly used to refer to the group, including "testudines" and "chelonians". While modern looking turtles likely appeared in the Jurassic period, a few primitive turtle fossils have been discovered from Triassic period deposits.

These turtles, which lived about 220 million years ago, differed greatly from modern turtles. Not only did they lack the proper shell of modern chelonians, they had teeth embedded in their upper and lower jaws.

Because of the unique body plan of testudines (a term that refers to all the various types of turtles, including marine, terrestrial and freshwater species), scientists have long debated the group's placement within the tree of life. Those swayed by morphological data believe that turtles are most closely aligned with Lepidosaurs (a group that includes snakes, lizards and tuataras). In part, this is based on the holes (fenestra) in the skulls of ancient turtles, which resemble those present in the skulls of lizards and snakes.

However, recent genetic studies of a wide variety of species has shed light on the placement of turtles within the tree of life, as well as the placement of individual species within the turtle umbrella. (Crawford, 2012)

According to this new research, turtles are the sister group to archosaurs (a group that includes crocodilians, birds and several extinct groups, such as non-avian dinosaurs). Lepidosaurs are the sister group to the ancestor of both archosaurs and testudines (a group named the archelosauria).

This means that the closest living relatives of turtles are crocodilians and birds, rather than snakes and lizards. Nevertheless, the two groups diverged from a common path hundreds of millions of years ago. So, while the two groups are each other's closest living relatives, they are not especially closely related.

As of August 2015, scientists currently recognize 341 living testudines, but this number fluctuates as new species are discovered, different species are synonymized and subspecies are elevated to the level of full species.

Snapping Turtles in the Tree of Life

According to genetic research, the basal split among living turtles occurs between two groups, called suborders. One group, called the Pleurodira, contains three living families and several extinct families, all of which inhabit South America, Australia, Southeast Asia or Africa. These turtles are easily recognized by their unusual neck construction, which causes them to withdraw their heads sideways, rather than straight back. A few examples of living pleurodine turtles include:

- Mata matas (*Chelus fimbriatus*)

- African helmeted turtles (*Pelomedusa subrufa*)
- Yellow-spotted river turtles (*Podocnemis unifilis*)

The other suborder of turtles – Cryptodira – includes the majority of the living species. Unlike pleurodines, which are restricted to the southern hemisphere, cryptodires live in both the northern and southern hemispheres. Examples of cryptodires include:

- Box turtles (*Terrapene* spp.)
- Galapagos tortoises (*Chelonoidis nigra*)
- Leatherback sea turtles (*Dermochelys coriacea*)

The term Cryptodira means "hidden neck," and refers to the fact that these turtles withdraw their heads straight back, rather than folding them to the side.

Within Cryptodira, snapping turtles (*Chelydra* spp.) are most closely related to the alligator snapping turtles (*Macrochelys temminckii*). The various common and alligator snapping turtle species are the only living representatives of the family Chelydridae. However, several extinct turtles are also placed in this family.

The family Chelydridae is the sister clade to the mud and musk turtles, with whom they share some morphological similarities.

Scientists debate the exact composition of the genus *Chelydra*. Some recognize only a single, highly variable and widespread species (*Chelydra serpentina*), while others recognize up to four subspecies within the genus:

- Northern snapping turtle (*Chelydra serpentina serpentina*)
- Mexican snapping turtle (*Chelydra serpentina rossignoni*)

- Florida snapping turtle (*Chelydra serpentina osceola*)
- Ecuadorian snapping turtle (*Chelydra serpentina acutirostris*)

However, as Florida snapping turtles and northern snapping turtles interbreed in several locations in southern Georgia and northern Florida, most taxonomists have synonymized the two – the Florida subspecies has thereby been discarded. (Feuer, 1971)

Most current researchers have elevated the northern and Mexican subspecies to the level of species (making them *Chelydra serpentina* and *Chelydra rossignoni* respectively). The status of the Ecuadorian snapping turtle is not well resolved.

While professional scientists and researchers may find them significant, the differences between the various snapping turtle species and subspecies are of little consequence to most hobbyists and keepers. What can be said of the biology, appearance and habits of one form generally applies to the others.

Chapter 4: The Environment of Snapping Turtles

Snapping turtles are largely generalists, who can survive in a wide variety of habitats, scattered over a very large range. Indeed, snapping turtles often thrive in habitats that prove inhospitable to other species.

Basic Geography

Geographic Range
In the broadest taxonomic sense, snapping turtles live from Canada to Ecuador. They are one of the most widespread reptilian species in all of North America.

Macro-habitat
Snapping turtles are capable of adapting to most aquatic habitats, but they seem to prefer slow bodies of water with soft substrates. They can be found in rivers, lakes and reservoirs, as well as smaller bodies, such as ponds and streams. They are quite adaptable to urban areas, and are often found within the limits of large cities.

Climate
Snapping turtles are tolerant of a wide range of temperatures. They become most active in the spring, summer and fall, although many observers have spotted snapping turtles swimming below ice.

Ecology

Vegetation
A variety of aquatic plants live throughout the range of snapping turtles. Snapping turtles are known to consume a significant amount of vegetation in their natural habitat, but

relatively little research has focused on the species that snapping turtles rely on for food.

The snapping turtles in some populations are known to shift their diet over the course of the year. In the spring, they concentrate on fish, amphibians and invertebrates. However, as summer arrives, and the aquatic plants begin to reappear, the turtles begin consuming vegetation almost exclusively.

It is likely that snapping turtles consume whatever is available in their pond or lake, rather than favoring one food source over another.

Prey Species
Snapping turtles are very effective predators, who consume a wide variety of prey species. Fish and invertebrates are among their most important prey, but they will also consume reptiles, amphibians, birds and mammals when the opportunity presents itself.

Predators
Snapping turtles have very few natural predators as adults. This is especially true while they are in the water.

Their size dissuades most predators, and most who are not daunted by their size surely pause when faced with the business end of an angry snapping turtle.

Alligators likely consume snapping turtles from time to time, and humans have been responsible for the deaths of countless snapping turtles over the millennia, but few other animals predate upon them regularly. They may also fall victim to larger snapping turtles (as well as their close relatives, the alligator snapping turtles).

Snapping turtles, particularly females intent on nesting, are often encountered while crossing roads.

Snapping turtles are more vulnerable on dry ground, and large predators, such as mountain lions, bears or large canines, may successfully kill and eat a few. However, the most dangerous encounters snapping turtles face are undoubtedly with humans or the cars they drive.

In contrast to the adults, young snapping turtles are eaten by a wide variety of predators. Other turtles – including other snapping turtles – represent a danger, as do large fish and wading birds. Otters, minks, raccoons and other nimble mammals can capture small snapping turtles lurking in the shallows.

Even before they hatch from their eggs, snapping turtles are at risk from countless nest-raiding predators. In fact, nest predation may be the most serious threat to would-be snapping turtles.

Other Associations

Snapping turtles harbor a number of internal parasites, including roundworms, tapeworms and protozoa. In the wild, these rarely build up to pathogenic levels, but the stress and confinement of captivity can cause the parasites to rise to dangerous levels.

Snapping turtles do not often bear external parasites, although they occasionally feature leaches attached to their skin or shell.

Chapter 5: Snapping Turtles as Pets: Captive Considerations

Now that you have a basic understanding of wild snapping turtles, it is important to examine their suitability for captivity and the responsibilities that go along with their care, before adding one to your family.

Snapping Turtle Suitability

When provided with suitable housing and care, snapping turtles thrive in captive environments. Many zoos, museums and educational institutions maintain them successfully.

Snapping turtles tend to be easy to feed, they adapt well to the presence of their keepers and they can adapt to a wide variety of husbandry protocols.

However, snapping turtles are not appropriate for most keepers. The reasons do not relate to the ability of the turtle to survive in captivity, but to the risks the keeper faces in keeping a potentially dangerous animal.

Put simply, beginners should not attempt to keep snapping turtles. They are large, often defensive animals that can cause very serious injuries.

Nevertheless, experienced keepers, with the resources, desire and dedication befitting such amazing animals, can successfully maintain these turtles for many years.

Snapping turtles – particularly captive bred individuals – quickly adjust to a life in captivity, although their defensive nature may never fade. They usually feed readily and adapt quickly to their captive habitat.

Snapping turtles are hardy creatures, who have relatively few common health problems. They are relatively tolerant of keeper errors and likely to thrive if provided with a suitable habitat, diet and maintenance regimen.

What You'll Need

To keep a snapping turtle as a pet, you must provide it with all of its needs. This includes:

- A suitable enclosure
- High-quality filter
- Appropriate substrate
- Cage furniture
- Proper lighting fixtures and bulbs
- Heating equipment
- Monitoring equipment (thermometers, etc.)
- Food
- Husbandry tools (tongs, etc.)
- Transport containers
- Cage cleaning equipment and supplies
- Water testing equipment

While every situation is different, a couple of fair scenarios are laid out in the following chart. These represent the initial costs of becoming a snapping turtle owner; they do not address on-going costs such as food and veterinary care.

Costs of Captivity

Inexpensive Option

Hatchling Snapping Turtle	$50 (£32)
Large Plastic Storage Box	$40 (£25)
Screen and Hardware for Lid	$10 (£6)
Heat Lamp Fixture and Bulbs	$20 (£13)
Digital Indoor-Outdoor Thermometer	$15 (£9)
Infrared Thermometer	$35 (£22)
Cage Furniture	$20 (£6)
Forceps, Misc.	$25 (£16)
Total	$215 (£140)

Moderate Option

Hypomelanistic Snapping Turtle	$500 (£326)
Cattle Trough	$75 (£49)
Custom Built Lid	$25 (£16)
Economy Filter	$100 (£65)
Heat Lamp Fixture and Bulbs	$20 (£13)
Digital Indoor-Outdoor Thermometer	$15 (£9)
Infrared Thermometer	$35 (£22)
Cage Furniture	$30 (£19)
Forceps, Misc.	$25 (£16)
Total	$825 (£539)

Premium Option

Amelanistic Snapping Turtle	$5,000 (£3266)
Custom Enclosure	$1000 (£653)
Radiant Heat Panel	$75 (£49)
Thermostat	$50 (£32)
Digital Indoor-Outdoor Thermometer	$15 (£9)
Infrared Thermometer	$35 (£22)
Cage Furniture	$100 (£19)
Forceps, Misc.	$25 (£16)
Total	$6,300 (£4115)

Understanding the Commitment
Myths and Misunderstandings

Before going further, it is important to distinguish between some of the myths and facts surrounding snapping turtles and their care.

Myth: Snapping turtles need friends or they will get lonely.

Fact: Snapping turtles live solitary lives in the wild, and only interact when breeding or engaging in male-male combat in the wild. Although some keepers house the turtles in pairs for breeding purposes, snapping turtles should usually be maintained singly in captivity. However, very young turtles may cohabitate relatively peacefully in communal tanks.

Myth: Reptiles grow in proportion to the size of their cage and then stop.

Fact: Reptiles do no such thing. Most healthy lizards, snakes and turtles grow throughout their lives, although the rate of growth slows with age. Placing them in a small cage in an attempt to stunt their growth is an unthinkably cruel practice, which is more likely to sicken or kill your pet than stunt its growth.

Myth: Snapping turtles must eat live food.

Fact: Snapping turtles must eat food, but they certainly do not care if it is alive or dead. It is usually easier to offer snapping turtles dead prey via long tongs or forceps. This reduces suffering on behalf of the prey and reduces the chances that your turtle will become injured during the process.

Myth: Reptiles have no emotions and do not suffer.

Fact: While turtles have very primitive brains, and do not have emotions comparable to those of higher mammals, they can absolutely suffer. Always treat reptiles with the same compassion you would offer a dog, cat or horse.

Myth: Snapping turtles are mean animals that like to bite people.

Fact: Snapping turtles would love nothing more than to be left alone. Snapping turtles avoid fights whenever possible, as the risk of injury or death is simply too great for them to take unnecessary risks. However, when they feel threatened, they will defend themselves vigorously.

Myth: If your snapping turtle is tame, he will never bite.

Fact: Even the most trustworthy snapping turtle should always be treated with respect. It only takes a second for your pet to become frightened, and react dangerously. Never place your hands or feet in front of a snapping turtle's head.

Myth: You can tell the age of a snapping turtle by counting the rings on its scutes.

Fact: While you can usually get a general idea of a snapping turtle's age by counting the rings on its scutes, the ring number rarely matches the age of the turtle precisely.

Chapter 6: Snapping Turtle Husbandry

Once equipped with a basic understanding of what snapping turtles are (Chapter 1 and Chapter 2), where they live (Chapter 3), what they do (Chapter 4) and the type of commitment they require (Chapter 5), you must start learning about their captive care.

Bear in mind that animal husbandry is an evolving pursuit. Keepers shift their strategies frequently as new information and ideas are incorporated into husbandry paradigms. There are few "right" or "wrong" answers, and what works in one situation may not work in another.

In all cases, you must strive to learn as much as possible about your animal, as well as how to provide it with the best quality of life.

The Enclosure

The first thing that you need to keep a snapping turtle as a pet is an enclosure – it is the defining characteristic of captivity!

Over the years, keepers have used a wide variety of enclosure types, each of which offers different benefits and drawbacks. Different turtle enthusiasts prefer different cage designs; some prefer inexpensive, but functional enclosures and place a premium on things like cost, durability and ease of maintenance, while other keepers desire to build the most visually impressive habitat possible. Still others may select an enclosure well suited for captive reproduction.

Similarly, keepers differ on the space requirements of turtles; some find relatively modest cage sizes to be sufficient, while others prefer to provide their turtles with larger accommodations.

Regardless of which side of the spectrum you fall on, you must always provide your pet with an enclosure that is large enough to meet the turtle's basic needs – minimally including sufficient room to establish thermal gradients, permit exercise and allow mental stimulation for the animal.

Consider all of the variables facing you and your pet, and select the cage size that best fits your circumstances.

While they spend much of their time walking along the bottom, snapping turtles are capable swimmers. Photo credit: © Nicholasrexrode, dreamstime.com – Large snapping turtle in pond photo.

Placement
The first major decision you must make with respect to the enclosure is its location. Specifically, you must decide whether you wish to keep your snapping turtle indoors or outdoors.

Because of their lightning needs, most turtles are best kept outdoors. While reptile lighting systems have come a long way in the last few decades, no lightbulb will ever be able to match the sun.

While little research into the specific lighting needs of snapping turtles has been completed, and it is certainly beneficial for them to have access to natural sunlight, they likely have less stringent lighting requirements than many other turtles.

Veterinarians, keepers and researchers are still piecing together the sunlight and turtle health puzzle. However, generally speaking, nocturnal reptiles need relatively little sun exposure. Further, reptiles that consume a large percentage of whole-animal prey typically need less sun exposure. Both of these factors suggest that snapping turtles may not benefit from access to direct sunlight as much as slider turtles (*Trachemys scripta* spp.) or leopard tortoises (*Geochelone pardalis*) do.

However, lighting is only one aspect of your turtle's care. You must also consider your pet's thermal environment and safety. Both of which are immeasurably easier to control indoors than outdoors.

Snapping turtles range throughout North, Central and South America; so many keepers live in places with similar climates as at least some populations of snapping turtles.

Snapping turtles kept outdoors are vulnerable to predators while small and nefarious humans throughout their lives. The list of potential suburban predators is daunting:

- Snakes
- Herons
- Raccoons

- Foxes
- Feral cats
- Feral dogs
- Coyotes
- Hawks
- Owls
- Minks
- Weasels
- Crows
- Ravens

Accordingly, to keep a small snapping turtle safe in an outdoor enclosure, you must often employ multiple safety features.

For example, a smooth wall 4 to 6 feet (1.2 to 1.8 meters) high surrounding the snapping turtle's habitat will likely keep out most snakes, but will do very little to keep out hawks and herons. You must also bury the wall at least 1 to 2 feet (30 to 60 centimeters) deep to keep digging predators, like dogs, from tunneling into the habitat.

In practice, the best method for keeping small turtles safe in an outdoor habitat is to construct a screen or mesh roof, which will allow sunlight and air to penetrate, with a weave tight enough to keep out snakes and other predators.

While large snapping turtles may be relatively safe from predators, determined humans may steal or harm your pet. Locks and security systems will reduce the chances of people accessing your pet, but they provide no guarantees.

Perhaps more alarmingly, your snapping turtle may inflict serious injuries on people who come into contact with him, whether their intentions were malevolent or not.

Given all of these challenges, most keepers elect to keep snapping turtles indoors.

Design and Materials

Snapping turtles are largely aquatic; they rarely crawl out onto dry land. Notable exceptions are during the process of egg deposition and when social or environmental challenges force them to relocate.

So, while you *should* provide males and *must* provide females with some area to crawl out of the water and deposit eggs (even if she is not kept with a male, female snapping turtles may produce egg clutches), the bulk of the enclosure should hold water.

Many commercial options are suitable for small snapping turtles, including aquaria and plastic turtle tubs. You can also repurpose items such as small, rigid swimming pools, plastic storage boxes or livestock water troughs to house small snapping turtles.

However, few commercial options are appropriate for large snapping turtles. A handful of commercial turtle tubs are marketed for "large" turtles, but few are adequately large for a mature snapping turtle.

A few manufacturers produce very large aquaria, which may be adequate for a large snapping turtle. Large plastic tubs are used in a variety of industries, and with sufficient searching, you may find one suitable for a large snapping turtle.

If none of these options are acceptable in your circumstances, you will be forced to construct (or solicit the construction of) a custom enclosure.

The fact that the enclosure will be full of water heavily influences your choice of materials. Glass, plastic and metal are the most obvious choices, although you can also use cement to create an enclosure. It is also possible to use wood, provided that you seal it well enough to hold water.

Each material has benefits and drawbacks. For example, glass is heavy and fragile, but it provides excellent visibility of your pet. Metal is extremely durable, but this is a material that requires special tools and knowledge to use.

Plastic is relatively durable, inexpensive and light, but it will become scratched over time. This can present challenges with keeping the tank clean, and scratches look terrible in transparent plastics (such as Plexiglas).

Size and Layout
In most cases, rectangular cage designs are superior to square or round cage designs. This is because the rectangular layout allows you to create a more effective thermal gradient in a given amount of space than a square or round layout does.

Additionally, rectangular enclosures provide a longer distance that the animal can travel before reaching a barrier, which is likely to promote better health and well-being.

Nevertheless, some keepers have had great success with cages of all shapes and configurations. As long as the turtle's needs are met, any configuration will work. To some extent, you will have to customize the enclosure to suit your home, given the scale of the enclosure.

Snapping turtle tanks should have a large footprint, but they need not be very deep, unless you live in a particularly cold region. Snapping turtles tend to spend most of their time in water only a couple of feet deep. While snapping turtles can certainly swim, they prefer to scoot around on the bottom of the tank.

Although snapping turtles are quite athletic (more so than is often supposed), try to make it easy on your turtle to move about the tank and haul out on dry land.

A sloped bottom is ideal, especially if there are plateaus at different depths. For example, you may construct a tank with a 4-square-foot area at about 3 feet (90 centimeters) of depth, connected to another, similar area at about 1 foot (30 centimeters) of depth. A sloped bottom should connect the two.

The proper size for a snapping turtle's cage is a subject of great debate. Many authorities present conflicting suggestions. In all cases, suggested cage sizes should be considered the minimum acceptable. Larger cages are almost always better.

Some experienced keepers advocate that enclosure should be five times the turtle's length long, three times the turtle's length wide, and at least two times the turtle's length deep. "Length" in these contexts refers to the length of the turtle's shell when measured in a straight line.

In other words, by this guideline, a 12-inch-long snapping turtle requires a 60-inch-long, 36-inch-wide, 24-inch deep enclosure. Likewise, a 2-inch-long snapping turtle would require a cage 10-inches-long, 6-inches-wide and 4-inches deep.

Other authorities recommend arbitrary tank sizes. Such keepers typically recommend starting with a 20- to 40-gallon aquarium, and moving up to 100-gallon aquariums upon maturity. However, it is important to understand that the capacity of the tank varies with the layout.

While a low-profile tank that contains 100 gallons of water may be large enough for a modest sized adult, a typical 100-gallon aquarium sold in pet stores has been designed for fish. Accordingly, such tanks have a very small footprint, but greater depth. Such cages are wholly inappropriate for large snapping turtles.

The Zoological Association of America requires turtles to have enclosures with an area equal to at least five times the length of the turtle's shell by two time the turtle's shell width. The pool area should be at least two times the shell length by two times the shell width. Additionally, an area of dry land equal to the size of the turtle's shell is required.

Therefore, if your snapping turtle's shell is 12 inches by 8 inches the entire enclosure must be a little over 6 square feet, while the pool must be about 2 2/3-square feet.

Substrate and Furniture

Now that you have decided what type of enclosure is right for you and your turtle, you can start placing the necessary items in the tank.

Most reptiles feel more secure in complex habitats than they do barren boxes with no visual barriers or items to investigate. Snapping turtles are no exception in this regard. However, you must strike a delicate balance between adding enough items to the enclosure to give your pet a sense of security and overcrowding the habitat, which makes maintenance more difficult and reduces the effective space available to your pet.

Substrates

In the wild, snapping turtles prefer areas with soft, muddy substrates. You can use sands designed specifically for aquarium use (play sand may lead to algae blooms) to recreate their natural habitat.

Alternatively, you can use gravel substrates. Gravel substrate provides anchoring opportunities for plants and looks attractive. However, it is possible for your turtle to swallow the rocks, which can lead to health problems. To address this concern, you can use gravel large enough that your turtle cannot ingest it.

Gravel substrates often keep the water looking cleaner, as debris tends to settle into the spaces between the small rocks, but this is misleading. While the debris does drift to the bottom of the tank, it still decomposes, releasing water-polluting compounds.

Once trapped in the gravel, this debris is not filtered out of the water. Eventually this requires the keeper to stir up the gravel and perform significant water changes to restore the water quality.

Given these challenges, many keepers elect to keep their snapping turtles in bare-bottomed tanks, with no substrate. While this is rarely as aesthetically pleasing as a gravel or sand substrate, it keeps the water much cleaner, which is more important to your turtle than the visual impact of the habitat.

In all cases, the bottom must be non-abrasive, so that your turtle does not suffer damage to its shell. If you use a cement pond, you will need to cover the bottom with suitable sand or gravel to avoid such problems.

This is one case in which bare-earth ponds excel, as the natural dirt bottom allows the turtle to dig into the bottom without damaging its shell.

Furniture

Snapping turtles do not often spend time in wide-open expanses of lakes and rivers. Instead, they prefer to live near structure of some type, which affords them some protection from predators.

Accordingly, you should add appropriately sized logs, branches or other hiding places, such as clay pots to the enclosure. Usually, your turtle will use one or more of these places as hiding spots.

Be careful that you do not restrict your turtle's activity by overcrowding the tank with rocks and sticks. It is also important to ensure such items are securely fastened, so your turtle does not topple them and damage the tank or injure itself.

Plants

Plants are another great addition to a snapping turtle enclosure. In addition to providing hiding places for your turtle, plants help to provide oxygen to the water. Plants also compete with algae for nutrients, which can help to reduce algae blooms.

Some keepers prefer to use artificial plants rather than live plants, as they require less care and frequent replacement. However, snapping turtles consume plants in the wild, and there is a chance they may attempt to consume artificial plants, which could lead to health problems.

Relatively little research has been conducted on the safety of different aquatic plants, but the following plants are likely safe for your snapping turtle. When in doubt, it is always wise to consult with your veterinarian before adding live plants to the enclosure.

However, some turtles tend to eat the plants in their enclosure, so some keepers prefer inedible aquatic plants.

- Water hyacinth
- Duckweed (*Lemna minor*)
- Water lettuce
- Water weed (*Elodea* spp.)
- (*Egeria densa*)
- Java fern (*Microsorium pteropus*)
- Java moss (*Vesicularia dubyana*)
- Hornwort (*Ceratophyllum demersum*)
- Red Ludwigia (*Ludwigia repens*)

Enclosure Climate

Ectothermic animals – often called "cold-blooded"– heat their bodies primarily via external sources, such as by basking in the sunlight or sitting on a warm rock. When they cannot reach suitable temperatures, they cannot digest their food effectively, move as quickly as necessary or perform other behaviors and bodily functions.

This can lead the animal to become dormant, such as occurs during the winter; in some cases it can cause the animal to become ill. Therefore, to maintain any ectothermic animal, such as a snapping turtle, you must provide suitable temperatures in the enclosure.

To ensure a suitable climate, you need high-quality heating devices as well as monitoring equipment. Additionally, you must arrange the heating equipment in such a way that you provide the captive with a range of temperatures.

Ideal Climate for Snapping Turtles

Snapping turtles are tolerant of a wide range of temperatures, but this does not mean that they will thrive at any temperature you choose.

Ideally, the water in the enclosure should be kept at temperatures of 75 to 80 degrees (23.8 to 26.6 degrees Celsius) and a basking site with surface temperatures of 90 to 95 degrees Fahrenheit (32.2 to 35 degrees Celsius).

The basking light should be turned off at night, and the cage temperature can be allowed to drop to room temperature during this period. It is also wise to lower the water temperatures about five to ten degrees Fahrenheit for about three months of the winter, but continue to provide a basking site.

Heating Devices

You can use any of several different types of heating devices. All have different pros and cons, which make a given device work in one scenario but not another.

You will need two different types of heating devices: One to heat the water and another to provide a warm basking spot.

CAUTION: Always use care when arranging and operating heating devices – especially when they are used near water. Always follow all manufacturer's instructions.

Heat Lamps

Heat lamps are the most common type of heating device used by turtle keepers to provide basking spots. Given the benefits of heat lamps, this makes good sense.

When reptile keepers refer to a "heat lamp", they mean a portable light socket surrounded by a shroud. A variety of different bulbs can be screwed into the receptacle. For example, some keepers prefer to use regular, incandescent light bulbs, while others prefer expanded-spectrum bulbs or mercury vapor bulbs.

Ceramic Heat Emitters

Ceramic heat emitters are used in place of a light bulb in a heat lamp fixture. However, unlike a light bulb, ceramic heat emitters produce no light. They only produce heat, which emanates from the ceramic.

On the plus side, most manufacturers claim that ceramic heat emitters are much more efficient than light bulbs. Additionally, as they produce no light, they can be used to heat the enclosure at night, without disturbing your pet's circadian rhythms.

However, ceramic heat emitters also have negative characteristics. Because they produce no light, you cannot tell if it is on or not by looking at it. This can lead to injuries if you accidentally touch it while it is on.

Ceramic heat emitters are also rather expensive, although when the efficiency and lifespan of the device is taken into consideration, this difference may become insignificant.

Radiant Heat Panels

Radiant heat panels are similar to heating pads, except that they are designed to project heat and warm things that are not in contact with the device. Additionally, radiant heat panels are generally placed on the ceiling or wall of an enclosure. This makes them very helpful for providing heat for a basking spot.

Radiant heat panels often cost more than heat lamps do, but they provide safer, more controlled heat. However, radiant heat panels must be used with a thermostat to ensure they do not overheat.

Aquarium Heater

Aquarium heaters are the best tools for keeping the water temperature within the proper range. These devices usually feature a coiled wire that heats up, a thermostat and a glass tube that encases the package.

Using an aquarium heater is relatively easy. Most feature an adjustable dial that allows you to set a predetermined temperature. You then place the heater in the enclosure water; monitor the temperatures for several days and make adjustments as necessary.

One drawback to using aquarium heaters with turtles is the possibility that the turtle will break the glass tube, and potentially electrocute itself. To prevent this from happening, a wire "cage" can be fitted around the heater, which will provide some protection from the turtle's strong legs and feet.

Heat Tape

Heat tape is plastic-covered electrical wire that is designed to heat up when current is applied. Heat tape is not appropriate for creating a basking spot, but it may help to keep the water temperatures at the desired level, if it is placed underneath the habitat. However, you must be sure to allow air to flow across the heat tape to prevent a dangerous buildup of heat.

Heat tape is largely inappropriate for beginning reptile keepers, as it must be wired by hand. Additionally, you must use heat tape with a thermostat or rheostat to maintain the proper temperatures. Care must be used when laying out heat tape, as improper placement can represent a fire hazard – always follow the manufacturer's instructions when assembling or using heat tape.

Heat Pads

Heating pads made for reptiles are generally constructed by enclosing a length of pre-wired heat tape in a plastic cover. Like heat tape, heat pads are not helpful for maintaining a basking spot, but they may help heat the water in the enclosure if safely attached to the outside of the cage. Be sure that the manufacturer's instructions permit this type of use before using a heat pad in this manner.

Heating pads should always be used with a thermostat or rheostat to maintain appropriate temperatures.

Heat Cables

Heat cables are long conducting wires that heat up when current is applied to them. Most heat cables are covered in plastic, which offers some protection from the elements, but they are not suitable for submersion.

However, heat cables can be used as heat tape or pads are, to heat the water. As always, follow the manufacturer's instructions.

Heated Rocks and Other Items

Heated rocks, branches, caves and other items were some of the earliest and most popular commercial heating devices for pet reptiles. They are made from a faux rock (or stick, etc.) and an internal heating element.

In previous decades, heated rocks garnered a bad reputation for burning reptiles. In some cases, this was due to faulty equipment, but in many others, it was due to keeper error.

These types of devices are not designed to raise the temperature of a pet reptile's habitat – they are merely designed to provide a localized basking spot. Unfortunately, many early keepers did not understand this, and so their pet reptiles wrapped tightly around these devices, while sitting in a woefully under heated cage.

Newer designs feature built-in rheostats or thermostats and are often constructed with better components. Nevertheless, they are inappropriate for aquatic turtles, and should be avoided.

Rheostats

Rheostats are akin to "volume controls" for heating devices. They work like lamp dimmer switches, as they reduce the amount of electricity reaching the heating device. This reduction in electricity reduces the amount of heat produced by the device.

Rheostats are helpful tools as they allow you to fine-tune the amount of heat supplied by a given device. However, you must still monitor the temperatures regularly, to ensure the cage temperatures stay within the desired range.

Thermostats

Thermostats are similar to rheostats, but they automatically adjust the amount of electricity reaching the heating device, in order to maintain a pre-selected temperature. Several different types of thermostats are available commercially.

Some work by simply switching the power to the heating device on and off. Others work by continually adjusting the amount of electricity reaching the device.

The former are called on-off thermostats while the later are termed pulse-proportional thermostats. On-off thermostats are only suitable for use with heat pads, radiant heat panels or heat tape.

While you must regularly check to ensure your thermostats are working, they are very helpful for maintaining proper cage temperatures, and they largely automate climate control.

Some thermostats feature a night-drop function, which allows you to program the unit to drop the temperatures by a preselected amount each night.

Thermostat Failure

All thermostats fail eventually. Whether this occurs a week after you purchase the unit or 30 years from now remains to be seen, but you must prepare for the possibility.

In a worst-case scenario, thermostat failure can lead to the death of your animals. This is not as likely to occur with aquatic animals, such as snapping turtles, but it is possible.

You can provide yourself with some protection from thermostat failure by purchasing a high-quality unit, crafted from quality components. However, even expensive thermostats can fail.

Another option is to use two thermostats, wired in series. To accomplish this, you must set the primary thermostat to the preferred temperature range for your animal. You then attach a second thermostat behind the first. Set this thermostat to a few degrees higher than the primary thermostat.

This way, when the primary thermostat fails, the secondary thermostat will allow the temperature to rise a few degrees, but will prevent the habitat from becoming dangerously warm.

Nighttime Heating

Snapping turtles are exposed to cooler nocturnal temperatures in the wild, and they will tolerate minor temperature drops during the night in captivity. However, it is important to avoid letting the temperature drop too low, as it may lead to illness.

Monitoring and Control Equipment

Maintaining an appropriate climate in your pet's enclosure often requires some trial and error, but this does not mean that you should blindly approach the task.

Instead, you must measure the cage temperatures, to ensure they are within the comfortable range for your pet. When keeping snapping turtles, this means using a digital thermometer to measure the water temperature and an infrared non-contact thermometer to measure the surface temperatures near the basking spot.

To use such a non-contact thermometer, you simply point it at the surface in question, click a button and read the surface temperature on a display. Most such units feature a red laser, which allows you to see precisely where you are aiming.

Thermal Gradients

One of the most basic principles of animal husbandry is to provide captives with a range of conditions, from which they can choose which is the most comfortable.

For example, it is wise to provide all captives – particularly reptiles and other ectothermic critters, who modify their temperature behaviorally – with a range of temperatures in their enclosure.

Keepers call this practice establishing a *thermal gradient*, but this sounds much more complicated than necessary. To create a thermal gradient, all you must do is place the heating device at one end of the enclosure. This way, temperatures will gradually fall with increasing distance from the heat source.

The area closest to the heat source essentially becomes a basking spot, while the far end of the cage serves as a cool retreat – intermediate temperatures allow your animal to fine-tune its internal temperature.

However, providing a thermal gradient for an aquatic turtle is a different endeavor. The tank filter will circulate the water, which will tend to cause the water to reach a uniform temperature.

Instead, the best way to provide a thermal gradient for aquatic turtles is by keeping the water temperature at the low end of their preferred temperature range and providing a basking site above the water's surface.

Differing Thermal Requirements
It is important to understand that small and young turtles are less tolerant of temperature extremes than large mature turtles are.

For the first year or two of your snapping turtle's life, try to keep the water temperature around 80 degrees Fahrenheit (26.6 degrees Celsius), and do not allow the basking site temperatures to exceed about 90 degrees Fahrenheit (32.2 degrees Celsius).

Additionally, do not allow the temperatures to drop very much at night or during the winter while your pet is under about 3 years of age.

Lighting

Most turtles require very specific lighting to remain healthy. When poor-quality light is provided, pet turtles may develop shell irregularities, bone degradation or kidney failure, among other problems.

Ideally, pet turtles should be afforded regular access to unfiltered sunlight. However, this is not always practical, especially for large and difficult-to-handle species, such as snapping turtles.

In lieu of natural sunlight, keepers should provide pet turtles with high quality, "full-spectrum" lighting. Full spectrum lighting refers to lights that produce not only visible light, but light in the UV portion of the range.

More specifically, turtles generally require lights that produce light in both the UVA and UVB portions of the range. UVA is defined as light between 320 and 400 nanometers, while UVB is defined as light between 290 and 320 nanometers.

UVC, which has wavelengths of between 100 and 290 nanometers, is destructive to cells, and is not produced by bulbs designed for reptile cages or general illumination.

UVA wavelengths have been shown to influence the vision and behavior of reptiles, although this has not specifically been shown to be true for snapping turtles. UVB wavelengths have widely been shown to allow reptiles to convert inactive vitamin D to the active form (Vitamin D3).

Vitamin D3 is crucial to the metabolism of calcium. When reptiles are deficient in vitamin D3, they tend to draw calcium from their bones. This leads to soft bones, and is termed metabolic bone disease. Often, the condition proves fatal, or becomes debilitating enough to require euthanasia.

Because they eat a lot of whole-prey, snapping turtles likely obtain a large portion of their D3 via their diets. After all, metabolic bone diseases are not seen as often in snapping turtles as they are herbivorous tortoises and slider turtles.

Further, snapping turtles do not bask as frequently or intensely as most other turtles, which may indicate UVB-derived vitamin D3 is not as important for these turtles.

Regardless of this possibility, it is wise to provide snapping turtles with full spectrum lighting to err on the side of caution. Once the symptoms of metabolic bone disease present themselves, the disease is often in an advanced state.

Most full spectrum lights are fluorescent bulbs. Both conventional and compact styles are available. Minimally, you must incorporate full spectrum bulbs over the basking site, but you can place them along the entire length of the enclosure if you prefer. However, if you choose to illuminate the entire tank with full-spectrum bulbs, be sure to offer the turtle refuges, where it can avoid the light.

The amount of UVB light emanating from the bulb dissipates rapidly with increasing distance from the lamp. This means that you must place the lights relatively close to the basking reptile – a maximum of about 12 inches (30 centimeters).

Full spectrum lights lose their ability to produce UVB over time, so you must replace them regularly. Follow the manufacturer's instruction regarding replacement schedule, but most lights last between 6 and 12 months.

Snapping turtles consume carrion when the opportunity arises.

Diet

Perhaps the easiest facet of snapping turtle husbandry is feeding. Snapping turtles are opportunistic omnivores, who readily consume almost any edible offerings.

CAUTION: Always use care when feeding snapping turtles. If offering food manually, use long tongs or forceps. Never feed snapping turtles by hand, or place your hands near feeding turtles.

Food Selection

The single most important aspect of feeding your snapping turtle (aside from minding your fingers) is to provide a diverse assortment of foods. This will ensure a well-rounded diet that is less likely to cause nutritional deficiencies.

As long as the prey size is adjusted to suit the turtle, adults and juveniles can be fed most of the same items. While snapping turtles consume large prey items in the wild, it is wise to feed captives items that they can swallow easily. Doing so will also prevent the tank from becoming fouled as quickly. As a rule of thumb, offer your snapping turtle prey items that are no longer than the distance between its eyes.

Some research suggests that hatchlings may imprint on the first food item they are offered, so there may be special value in providing hatchlings with a diverse array of foods.

Some acceptable food items for snapping turtles include the following:

Insects

- Crickets
- Mealworms
- Superworms
- Roaches
- Wax worms
- Silkworms
- Grasshoppers

Other Invertebrates

- Earthworms
- Red wigglers
- Leaches
- Snails
- Crayfish
- Shrimp
- Crabs
- Squid
- Octopus

Fish

- Trout
- Anchovies
- Sardines
- Catfish

- Salmon
- Herring
- Cod
- Flounder
- Feeder minnows

Rodents

- Mice
- Rats
- Gerbils
- Hamsters

Fruits

- Strawberries
- Grapes
- Melon
- Blueberries
- Blackberries
- Bananas
- Squash
- Sweet peppers
- Pumpkin

Vegetables

- Collard greens
- Mustard greens
- Turnip greens
- Greenleaf lettuce
- Spinach
- Kale
- Endive
- Green beans
- Sweet potato

Some keepers like to maintain a small population of fish in the aquarium, which provides their turtle with a constant supply of food. Leaving live fish in the tank also provides some exercise and mental stimulation for your turtle.

Avoid feeding your turtle goldfish, as they frequently harbor parasites, which they may pass to your turtles. Instead, opt for feeder minnows or small freshwater fish.

While the occasional frozen fish is unlikely to harm your turtle, avoid making frozen fish a staple dietary item, as this can lead to nutritional deficiencies. Instead, opt for human-grade, fresh fish.

Only offer previously killed rodents to your snapping turtle. This not only prevents unnecessary suffering for the rodent, but it reduces the chances that your turtle will suffer an injury from a fighting rodent.

Commercial turtle pellets are also helpful for feeding young snapping turtles, although large adults may not show any interest. However, avoid getting into the habit of offering commercial pellets too frequently; always be sure to rotate a variety of food items, so that your turtle benefits from a well-rounded diet.

Feeding Frequency

Generally speaking, feeding frequencies should decrease with advancing age. Young turtles can be fed four to six times per week, while mature adults only require one to three feedings per week.

The best way to ensure that you are feeding a young turtle enough food is by measuring it frequently. Healthy young turtles should grow month after month.

To ensure you are feeding a mature adult enough, it should grow slowly, if at all. It is easier and more helpful to weigh large turtles, while it is easier to measure the length of small turtles.

Vitamin and Mineral Supplementation
Some keepers apply vitamin or mineral supplements to their food items to ensure their turtle does not suffer from any nutritional deficiencies.

While vitamin and mineral supplements are helpful in some contexts, they can also cause problems if they are overused. Calcium, for example, is very harmful in high doses.

Accordingly, it is important to consult with your veterinarian before starting a supplementation scheme.

Water Quality
As with fish, aquatic turtles require clean, healthy water to remain healthy. While most turtles are not as sensitive to water conditions as fish are, poor water quality can lead to health problems.

Proper filtration and periodic water changes will keep most of the relevant water quality parameters within tolerances, but you may need water conditioners and other chemicals to keep the pH correct and to alleviate any chlorine or chloramine in the water.

Important Aspects of Water Quality
Be sure that you address each of the following water quality issues to keep your turtle's tank water clean.

- **Chlorine / Chloramine** – Chlorine and chloramine are used as antibacterial agents in tap water. You can remove or neutralize both agents with water conditioners sold at pet stores.

- **Ammonia / Nitrites / Nitrates** – Ammonia levels in the tank will rise over time, as your turtle releases waste into the water. Ammonia is toxic, but fortunately, nitrifying bacteria can convert ammonia into nitrates. Nitrates are also toxic, but different bacteria can convert nitrates into nitrites, which are relatively harmless. The bacteria necessary to complete the process will form naturally on your filter media. However, it is important to monitor the levels of ammonia, nitrates and nitrites to keep the water as healthy as possible; you can do this with a water test kit.
- **pH** – Snapping turtles adapt best to slightly acidic water. Strive to keep the pH between 6.5 and 7. A water test kit will allow you to monitor the pH. Your local pet store will have products available to adjust the pH in either direction, as necessary.

Filtration

Unless you plan to perform water changes several times each week, a high-quality water filter is necessary for snapping turtle maintenance.

Modern filters treat the water in three different ways. The first stage in the process, called mechanical filtration, removes the particulate matter from the tank. The second stage uses bacteria living on the filter media to convert ammonia and its derivatives into safer substances – this is called biological filtration. Finally, the water passes through an activated carbon filter, which bonds with most chemicals passing through it. This step is referred to as chemical filtration.

The style of the water filter is not terribly important; some keepers prefer canister-style filters, while others prefer units that hang on the back of the aquarium. Either style will work – the important consideration is the capacity of the filter.

Filters are rated for varying quantities of water. For example, you may see filters rated for 100-gallon aquariums and others rated for 20-gallon aquariums. These ratings work well for aquariums containing fish, but because turtles create a considerable amount of waste, it is wise to select a filter rated for two to three times the size of your turtle's tank. In other words, if your pet lives in a 50-gallon habitat, purchase a filter rated for 100- or 150-gallon aquariums.

You will need to clean the filter unit regularly to keep it working at peak efficiency. Avoid using any chemicals to do so; instead, simply rinse the unit and filter cartridges with water. Be sure to use "dirty" tank water to rinse the biological filter cartridge, as chlorinated water will kill the bacteria.

Water Changes
While your filter will help keep the tank water clean, few models are effective enough to keep the water clean without a little help. This help comes in the form of partial water changes.

To perform a partial water change, begin by preparing enough new water to replace about half of the water in the tank. Treat the water as necessary to remove or neutralize the chlorine or chloramine, and allow it to warm to room temperature. Then, remove and discard approximately half of the water in the tank. Finally, add the new water to the tank to complete the partial water change.

You can use a bucket to bail water from the turtle tank, but a siphon hose will make the project much easier. Complete a partial water change about once every week or two to keep the water clean and reduce the workload for the tank filter.

Monitoring and Maintenance

Once you have set up the habitat, you must work to keep it habitable for your pet. Most illnesses in captive reptiles spring from inappropriate husbandry (particularly the failure to keep the habitat suitably clean), so be vigilant about maintaining the habitat to avoid such problems.

Cleaning Techniques and Supplies

Some of the things you may need to maintain the habitat include:

- Paper towels
- Soap-free scrub pads
- Heavy-duty, plastic bristled scrub brush
- Wire scrub brush
- Bleach
- Measuring cups
- Spray bottles
- Long-handled scrubbing tool
- Aquarium net
- Razor blades

Maintenance Schedule

Try to establish a regular maintenance routine. Some tasks are necessary on a daily basis, while other tasks can be performed less frequently.

Daily

- Visually inspect the habitat and turtle, looking for any problems with the habitat or health concerns.
- Measure the water temperature and the surface temperature of the basking spot.
- Ensure that the filter is working properly.

Weekly

- Skim any debris from the surface with a net.
- Check all tubes for signs of leaks or wear.
- Siphon out any visible debris or organic matter.
- Perform a 25 to 50 percent water change.

Monthly

- Break down the entire habitat. Empty the water completely. Clean out the filter, but do not destroy the bacterial colony (place the filter media in a bucket containing the "old" tank water while you clean the unit). Scrub any algae off the sides of the aquarium and furniture.
- Replace plants or cage furniture as necessary.
- Weigh and measure your turtle. This is particularly important with young turtles, so that you can monitor their growth. If your turtle is mature, healthy and aggressive, you can weigh and measure it less frequently.

Annually

- Change the full-spectrum bulbs (some bulbs require replacement every 6 months – consult the manufacturer's instructions).
- Inspect all of the electrical cords, light fixtures, filter tubes and all other equipment for signs of wear.

Records

Proper record keeping is a crucial aspect of reptile husbandry. Unfortunately, too many keepers neglect this simple and important practice.

Written records allow you to note trends, anticipate problems before they occur and learn from prior mistakes. They also prove invaluable if your turtle falls ill. By reviewing your husbandry records with your veterinarian, you may be able to figure out why a given health problem is occurring.

You can keep records in virtually any way you like. Some prefer to use elaborate record-keeping software packages, while others prefer to take handwritten notes, as with a journal.

Either of these options – or any other option that suits your needs – is acceptable. The important thing is that you keep records.

While you can never record too much data, there are a few types of data that are important, and should not be neglected. For example, you should always record the source of the turtle, the date on which you acquired the turtle, and the weight (and length if possible) the turtle was at the time of acquisition.

A few record-keeping examples are on the following pages.

ID Number	44522	Genus: Species/Sub:	Chelydra serpentina	Gender DOB:	Male 9/20/14	CARD #2
6.30.15 Mouse	7.07.15 50% water change	7.14.15 50% water change	7.21.15 50% water change	7.26.15 12 crickets		
7.01.15 Pellets	7.10.15 Kale leaves	7.16.15 2 Crayfish	7.23.15 10 minnows	7.30.15 50% water change		
7.04.15 2 Grapes, Pellets	7.12.15 Mouse	7.19.15 12 minnows	7.25.15 2 Cantaloupe cubes			

Date	Notes
6-24-13	Acquired ""Snappy" the snapping turtle from a breeder named Mark at the in-town reptile expo. Mark explained that snappy's scientific name is Chelydra serpentina. Cost was $75. Mark was not sure what sex Snappy was. He said he hatched in October, but he does not know the exact date.
6-25-13	I have decided to consider Snappy a boy until he gets big enough to be sure. I purchased a 40-gallon aquarium, canister filter, screened lid and heat lamp at the pet store. Bought the thermometer at the hardware store next door and ordered a non-contact thermometer online. I bought some fake plants at the pet store to decorate his cage.
6-27-13	Fed Snappy a dozen minnows. He ate seven of them, but I am keeping the rest in the tank until he gets hungry again.
6-28-13	Well, Snappy must have finished the minnows last night, because they are all gone!
7-1-13	Snappy was looking hungry, so I gave him some blueberries. He had trouble figuring out how to eat them at first, but eventually he got it.
7-8-13	Performed a 50 percent water change for the tank – he certainly makes his water messy!

Chapter 7: Acquiring a Snapping Turtle

Now that you have decided to get a snapping turtle, and you understand the care it requires, it is time to find your pet. Modern reptile enthusiasts can acquire snapping turtles from a variety of sources, each with a different set of pros and cons.

PRO TIP: It is easy to get over excited about the potential of a new pet, which can lead to hasty decisions and regret. Take your time and select the perfect snapping turtle for you. You will have your snapping turtle for the next several decades; you can wait a few weeks to find the ideal companion.

Pet Stores

Pet stores are a common source for many beginning turtle keepers, but they are not always the best place to purchase your new pet.

The benefits of shopping at a pet store are that they usually have all of the equipment to care for your new lizard, including cages, heating devices and food items. You will usually be able to inspect the turtle up close before purchase. In some cases, you may be able to choose from more than one specimen.

Many pet stores provide health guarantees for a short period, which provides you with some recourse if your new pet turns out to be ill. However, pet stores are retail establishments, and as such, you will pay more than you will from a breeder. Pet stores do not often know the pedigree of the animals they sell, nor are they likely to know the turtle's date of birth, or other pertinent information.

The drawbacks to purchasing a turtle from a pet store relate to the amount of expertise and knowledge of the staff. While some pet stores concentrate on reptiles and may have a staff capable of providing them with proper care, many turtles languish while living in pet stores.

It is also worth considering the increased exposure to pathogens that pet store animals endure, given the constant flow of animals through the facility.

Reptile Expos

Reptile expos are often excellent places to acquire new animals. Reptile expos often feature resellers, breeders and retailers in the same room, all selling various types of turtles and other reptiles.

Often, the prices at such events are quite reasonable and you are often able to select from many different turtles. However, if you have a problem, it may be difficult to find the seller after the event is over.

Breeders

Breeders are the best place for most novices to shop for turtles. Breeders generally offer unparalleled information and support after the sale. Additionally, breeders often know the species well, and are better able to help you learn the husbandry techniques for the animal.

The disadvantage of buying from a breeder is that you must often make such purchases from a distance, either by phone or via the internet. Breeders often have the widest selection of turtles, and are often the only place to find rare forms and truly spectacular specimens.

Classified Advertisements

Newspaper and website classified advertisements sometimes include listings for turtles. While individuals, rather than businesses generally post these, they are a viable option to monitor. Often these sales include the turtle and all of the associated equipment, which is convenient for new keepers. However, be careful to avoid purchasing someone else's "problem" (i.e. a sick or maladapted turtle).

Selecting Your Turtle

Not all turtles are created equally – you want to be careful in selecting the best specimen you can find. While you can consider color or other aesthetic qualities in your selection process, they should be minor concerns. Only select turtles that appear healthy.

Health Checklist

Never purchase a snapping turtle displaying any of the following signs or symptoms:

- Lumps, swellings or ulcers
- Puffy or closed eyes
- Shell deformations or wounds
- Limb or tail deformations
- Overgrown beak
- Discharge from the eyes
- Discharge from the nostrils or mouth
- Discharge from the vent

If possible, observe the turtle swimming and walking on the ground. Healthy snapping turtles appear strong and surprisingly light on their feet. They swim well, although they may prefer to walk along the bottom, which is not indicative of illness.

Most snapping turtles will react defensively to humans who get too close, but occasional specimens appear to tolerate more interaction than others do. Accordingly, the animal's disposition is not a particularly helpful criterion to consider.

The Gender

Whenever possible, select male snapping turtles for pets. While it is true that males grow to slightly larger sizes than females do, which is not always ideal, males do not present any of the reproductive-related challenges females do.

Female turtles – even those who are not housed with males – may produce eggs. If they cannot find a suitable egg deposition site, they may become egg bound. This can necessitate expensive and invasive surgeries, or lead to death.

The Age

Most snapping turtles offered for sale in the reptile hobby are hatchling or year-old animals. However, adult snapping turtles appear on the market from time to time. Unless you have considerable experience caring for large, potentially dangerous turtles, always purchase snapping turtles that are young and small. This will give you some time to learn your pet's temperament and behavior, while refining your skills.

Chapter 8: Interacting with Your Snapping Turtle

Generally speaking, the less you touch your snapping turtle the better. Contact with a large predator (such as yourself) may cause the turtle stress, which can lead to illness and maladaptation.

However, you need to observe your turtle for signs of illness regularly, and this will occasionally necessitate directly handling the animal.

Handling a snapping turtle is a serious task that demands your full attention. A momentary lapse in concentration can lead to serious injuries.

Before attempting to handle your turtle, be sure that the room is calm. Have young children leave the room, and exclude pets from the area.

Ensure another adult is on hand before handling large snapping turtles. If bitten, you will likely need help to free yourself.

CAUTION: Never attempt to handle a snapping turtle without first obtaining training from a knowledgeable keeper. The following methods are provided for informational purposes only.

Handling Snapping Turtles

Different techniques are necessary for handling snapping turtles of different sizes. Hatchlings are relatively easy to hold, but medium and large adults require entirely different techniques.

Suspending a turtle by its tail can lead to spinal injuries. Although you can use the tail to help maintain balance while you are holding the animal, never use a turtle's tail to support its body weight, regardless of its size.

Holding 1- to 2-inch-long Snapping Turtles

Very small snapping turtles are often less inclined to bite than their larger counterparts are. Should they decide to bite, the consequences are usually minor. However, it is always wise to avoid bites from any animal, as infections are always possible when the skin is broken.

The best way to hold these very small turtles is by placing your index finger on top of the animal's carapace and placing your thumb under its plastron. Do not pinch the shell too firmly, as young turtle shells lack the rigidity of adult shells.

Holding 3- to 6-inch-long Snapping Turtles

By the time your snapping turtle has become 3 to 6 inches (7 to 15 centimeters), they are capable of inflicting rather serious wounds. From this size onward, you must use great care when handling your pet.

The easiest way to hold turtles of this size is to lift them from behind. Place your thumb on the rear portion of the turtle's carapace, and place your fingers on the rear portion of the turtle's plastron. Allow the tail to protrude from between your fingers.

Holding 7- to 12-inch-long Snapping Turtles

At a point, your snapping turtle will become large or heavy enough that it is difficult to hold it with one hand. In these cases, you can simply use the same technique as before, but instead of using one hand; use both hands to support its weight.

The tail will protrude from between your hands, but you will still be placing your fingers on its plastron and your thumbs on its carapace.

A secondary benefit of this holding method is that it can help keep your hands away from the turtle's claws, which will often be flailing in an attempt to gain a foothold.

Holding Very Large Snapping Turtles

Handling very large snapping turtles is often challenging. In addition to the pugnacious disposition characteristic of most snapping turtles, very large specimens are quite heavy.

You can hold very large snapping turtles using the same two-handed method as described above; but if the turtle is slippery or heavy, this may not be easy.

One of the best methods for holding large snappers is to grasp the animal's tail with one hand, while lifting the animal with a hand placed on the rear of the turtle's plastron. When performing this technique, avoid pulling on the animal's tail, which simply provides a way to balance the animal. The hand on the turtle's plastron should support the animal's weight almost entirely.

Alternatively, some keepers prefer to lift and hold snapping turtles in the same manner in which alligator snapping turtles are held. For this technique, one hand is slid forward along the turtle's carapace. When the hand reaches the front edge, the fingers curl around the carapace. The other hand grasps the turtle at the back of the shell.

While it is true that alligator snapping turtles can be held safely in this fashion, the technique is not safe to use with common snapping turtles. Snapping turtles have smaller, nimbler heads than their larger cousins do, and they tend to bite in slightly different ways.

Whereas alligator snapping turtles slowly wave their open mouths, waiting for something to come within biting range; common snapping turtles often keep their heads retracted, waiting to snap at anything they think they can reach.

Though they may have trouble getting their heads turned around tightly enough to bite fingers wrapped around the front portion of their carapaces, they can certainly inflict a serious bite while you are moving your hand along its back into position.

Common snapping turtles are quite capable of reaching back over their carapaces and biting the hand that touches them. Usually they can reach back about half the length of their shell, meaning that your hands are very vulnerable to a bite while trying to get into position to lift a turtle in this fashion.

Whichever method you choose, be sure to keep its head far enough from your face, legs and body to avoid potential bites.

Transporting Snapping Turtles

From time to time, it will be necessary to transport your snapping turtle. When doing so, you must keep the turtle protected from injury, within the appropriate temperature range and protected from sources of stress.

The best way to do so is by placing your turtle in a large plastic storage box, filled with a soft layer of newspaper. Opaque boxes will keep your turtle calmer, while transparent boxes will allow you to observe the animal without opening the lid.

Be sure to drill a few ventilation holes on each of the container's vertical sides so that your pet can breathe easily.

In The Event of a Bite

Despite your best efforts, you may one day find yourself with part of your body in a snapping turtle's mouth.

This is obviously a frightening potentiality, but because extricating yourself from the angry reptile's jaws is often difficult, you must do your best to remain calm and act deliberately.

All turtles are individuals, and all circumstances are unique, but often, the quickest way to get a snapping turtle to open its jaws is to release it into the water. This will make your turtle feel safe, at which time he will release your hand or finger and beat a hasty retreat.

If this fails to work – or you suffer a bite on your torso, neck or face, which may be difficult to get into the water – you must try to pry the turtle's jaws open. Using a flat tool, such as a flathead screwdriver, try to slide the tip between the turtle's jaws and then press down on the tool's handle, as you would a pry bar.

With luck, the turtle will release its grip, at which time you can pull yourself free. Stay alert, as the turtle may release the bite only to bite down again (potentially giving you a new wound).

If you are unable to get the turtle to release its grip using either of these techniques, travel to the hospital or your doctor for assistance. It may not be possible to remove the turtle without harming or killing it, so prepare yourself accordingly.

After any bite, regardless of the severity or lack thereof, wash the wound with warm, soapy water and apply an over-the-counter antiseptic. If the wound is severe, see your doctor immediately.

Hygiene

Turtles often carry various strains of *Salmonella* bacteria, as well as other harmful pathogens. While these bacteria rarely cause illness in the turtles, they can make humans – particularly those with compromised immune systems – very ill. In tragic cases, death can result from such infections.

Accordingly, it is imperative to employ sound hygiene practices when caring for a pet turtle. In general, this means:

- Always wash your hands with soap and warm water following any contact with your pet, the enclosure or items that have contacted either.
- Never wash turtle cages, furniture or tools in sinks or bathtubs used by humans.
- Never perform any husbandry tasks in kitchens or bathrooms used by humans.
- Keep high-risk individuals, such as those who are less than 5 years of age, elderly, pregnant or otherwise immunocompromised, away from captive turtles and their habitats.

Chapter 9: Snapping Turtle Health

Snapping turtles are remarkably hardy animals, who often remain healthy in circumstances that would cause other species to fall ill. In fact, most illnesses that befall pet snapping turtles result from improper husbandry, and are therefore, entirely avoidable.

Nevertheless, snapping turtles, like most other reptiles, often fail to exhibit any symptoms that they are sick until they have reached an advanced state of illness. This means that prompt action is necessary at the first hint of a problem. Doing so provides your pet with the greatest chance of recovery.

While proper husbandry is solely in the domain of the keeper, and some minor injuries or illnesses can be treated at home, veterinary care is necessary for many health problems.

Finding a Suitable Vet

While any veterinarian – even one who specializes in dogs and cats – may be able to help you keep your pet happy, it is wise to find a veterinarian who specializes in treating reptiles. Such veterinarians are more likely to be familiar with your pet species and be familiar with the most current treatment standards for reptiles.

Nevertheless, reptile-oriented veterinarians are also more likely to be comfortable dealing with large, potentially aggressive pets, such as snapping turtles.

Some of the best places to begin your search for a reptile-oriented veterinarian include:

- Veterinary associations (see Chapter 12)
- Local pet stores
- Local colleges and universities

It is always wise to develop a relationship with a qualified veterinarian before you need his or her services. This way, you will already know where to go in the event of an emergency, and your veterinarian will have developed some familiarity with your pet.

When to See the Vet

Most conscientious keepers will not hesitate to seek veterinary attention on behalf of their pet. However, veterinary care can be expensive for the keeper and stressful for the kept, so unnecessary visits are best avoided.

If you are in doubt, call or email your veterinarian and explain the problem. He or she can then advise you if the problem requires an office visit or not.

However, you must always seek prompt veterinary care if your pet exhibits any of the following signs or symptoms:

- Traumatic injuries, such as lacerations, burns, broken bones, cracked shells or puncture wounds
- Sores, ulcers, lumps or other deformations of the skin
- Intestinal disturbances that do not resolve within 48 hours
- Drastic change in behavior
- Inability to deposit eggs

Remember that reptiles are perfectly capable of feeling pain and suffering, so apply the golden rule: If you would appreciate medical care for an injury or illness, it is likely that your pet does as well.

Common Health Problems

The following are some of the most common health problems that afflict snapping turtles. Be alert for any signs of the following maladies, and take steps to remedy the problem.

Respiratory Infections

Respiratory infections are some of the most common illnesses that afflict turtles and other captive reptiles.

The most common symptoms of respiratory infections are discharges from the nose or mouth; however, lethargy, inappetence and behavioral changes (such as basking more often than normal) may also accompany respiratory infections.

Myriad causes can lead to this type of illness, including communicable pathogens, as well as, ubiquitous, yet normally harmless, pathogens, which opportunistically infect stressed animals.

Your turtle may be able to fight off these infections without veterinary assistance, but it is wise to solicit your vet's opinion at the first sign of illness. Some respiratory infections can prove fatal and require immediate attention.

Your vet will likely obtain samples, send of the samples for laboratory testing and then interpret the results. Antibiotics or other medications may be prescribed to help your turtle recover, and your veterinarian will likely encourage you to keep the turtle's stress level low, and ensure his enclosure temperatures are ideal.

In fact, it is usually a good idea to raise the temperature of the basking spot upon first suspecting that your turtle is suffering from a respiratory infection. Elevated body temperatures (such as those that occur when mammals have fevers) help the turtle's body to fight the infection, and many will bask for longer than normal when ill.

Metabolic Bone Disease

Metabolic bone disease (MBD) is a complicated phenomenon that befalls turtles who are provided with insufficient calcium or insufficient amounts of the active form of vitamin D (D3), which is necessary for calcium utilization.

A well-rounded, diverse diet with plenty of whole-body prey helps to ensure your pet receives enough calcium. Additionally, many keepers supplement their turtle's food items with calcium powders. However, it is important to consult with your veterinarian to devise a suitable supplementation schedule, as providing too much calcium can be just as problematic as providing too little.

A balanced diet will provide your turtle with plenty of inactive vitamin D. To allow your pet to convert this into the active form, you must provide it with exposure to ultraviolet radiation (specifically UVB). This can be accomplished either by housing your turtle outdoors and allowing them to bask in natural sunlight, or by illuminating their enclosure with full spectrum lights that produce light in the UVB portion of the spectrum.

When deprived of proper lighting, the calcium levels in the turtle's blood fall. This causes the turtle's body to draw calcium from the bones (including the shell) to rectify the problem.

As calcium is removed from the bones, they become soft and flexible, rather than hard and rigid. This can lead to broken bones or disfigurement, which can leave your turtle unable to eat, walk or swim.

Advanced cases of MBD are rarely treatable, and euthanasia is often the only humane option. However, when caught early and treated aggressively, some of the symptoms of the disease can be stopped. Accordingly, it is of the upmost importance to seek veterinary care at the first sign of MBD.

Shell Rot

Shell rot is a catchall term for a variety of maladies related to a turtle's shell. Shell rot normally takes the form of lesions or ulcers; sometimes, a small amount of fluid may leak from the wounds.

Shell rot may occur because of a systematic infection or as a local phenomenon. Bacteria or fungi may be the primary cause of the problem, or injuries may provide an opportunity for pathogens to colonize the tissues.

Shell rot is usually treatable with prompt veterinary care, so always see your veterinarian at the first sign of problems.

Parasites

Parasites are rare among captive-bred snapping turtles, but they are often present in wild specimens. Parasites rarely become problematic for wild turtles, unless they become injured, stressed or ill.

Most internal parasites cause intestinal problems, such as runny or watery stools, vomiting or decreased appetites. Your veterinarian can collect blood or stool samples from your turtle, analyze them to determine what parasites, if any, are present, and prescribe medications to clear the infestation. Often, multiple treatments are necessary to eradicate the parasites completely.

External parasites afflict wild living snapping turtles on occasion, usually in the form of leeches. Most leeches will not cause harm and they can be easily removed by your veterinarian.

Anorexia

Snapping turtles are voracious predators, who rarely pass up the chance to consume calories. However, they may refuse food if ill, if kept in suboptimal temperatures (including seasonally cool temperatures, such as occur during the winter) or are preoccupied by breeding.

Refusing a meal or two is not cause for alarm, but if your turtle refuses food for longer than this, be sure to review your husbandry practices. If the turtle continues to refuse food without an obvious reason for doing so, consult your veterinarian.

Injuries

Snapping turtles can become injured in myriad ways, including battles with cagemates, overly zealous breeding attempts, or by sustaining burns from heaters. While snapping turtles are likely to heal from most minor wounds without medical attention, serious wounds will necessitate veterinary assistance.

Your vet will likely clean the wound, make any repairs necessary (shell patches, sutures, etc.) and prescribe a course of antibiotics to help prevent infection. Be sure to keep the water and enclosure as clean as possible during the healing process.

Egg Binding

Egg binding occurs when a female is unable or unwilling to deposit her eggs in a timely fashion. If not treated promptly, death can result.

The primary symptoms of egg binding are similar to those that occur when a gravid turtle approaches parturition. Egg bound turtles may appear panicked or repeatedly try to escape their enclosure. However, unlike turtles who will deposit eggs normally, egg bound turtles continue to exhibit these symptoms without producing a clutch of eggs.

As long as you are expecting your turtle to lay eggs, you can easily monitor her behavior and act quickly if she experiences problems. However, if you are not anticipating a clutch, this type of problem can catch you by surprise.

Prolapse

Prolapses occur when a turtle's intestines protrude from its vent. This is an emergency situation that requires prompt treatment. Fortunately, intestinal prolapse is not terribly common among turtles.

You will need to take the animal to the veterinarian, who will attempt to re-insert the intestinal sections. Sometimes sutures will be necessary to keep the intestines in place while the muscles regain their tone.

Try to keep the exposed tissue damp, clean and protected while traveling to the vet. It is likely that this problem is very painful for the animal, so try to keep its stress level low during the process.

Quarantine

Quarantine is the practice of isolating animals to prevent them from transferring diseases between themselves.

If you have no other pet reptiles (particularly turtles), quarantine is unnecessary. However, if you already maintain other turtles (especially other snapping turtles) you must provide all new acquisitions with a separate enclosure.

At a minimum, quarantine all new acquisitions for 30 days. However, it is wiser still to extend the quarantine period for 60 to 90 days, to give yourself a better chance of discovering any illness present before exposing your colony to new, potentially sick, animals. Professional zoological institutions often quarantine animals for six months to a year. In fact, some zoos keep their animals in a state of perpetual quarantine.

Chapter 10: Breeding

Many – if not most – turtle keepers are eventually bitten by the captive breeding bug. Determined to produce a clutch of adorable hatchlings, these keepers acquire specimens of each sex and begin waiting for eggs.

This is a natural progression for keepers, and, when carried out in responsible fashion, a boon for the species, as captive breeding projects help alleviate pressure on wild populations.

However, irresponsible breeders often cause greater problems for the hobby.

Such breeders often set out with the explicit goal of profiting from their turtles, rather than enjoying their pets in their own right. This ensures failure for the vast majority of people that try to breed turtles for profit.

Pre-Breeding Considerations

Before you set out to breed snapping turtles, consider the decision carefully. Unfortunately, few keepers realize the implications of breeding their turtles before they set out to do so.

Ask yourself if you will be able to:

- Provide adequate care for a pair of adult turtles
- Provide the proper care for the female while gravid
- Afford emergency veterinary services if necessary
- Incubate 30 or more eggs in some type of incubator
- Provide housing for 30 or more hatchlings
- Provide food for 30 or more hatchlings

- Dedicate the time to caring for 30 or more hatchlings
- Find new homes for 30 or more hatchlings

If you cannot answer each of these questions affirmatively, you are not in a position to breed snapping turtles responsibly.

Legal Issues

Before deciding to breed your snapping turtles, you must investigate the relevant laws in your area. Some municipalities require turtle breeders to obtain licenses, insurance and permits, although others do not.

Additionally, because they are potentially dangerous and capable of colonizing alien habitats, snapping turtle ownership is prohibited in some locations. Others allow their possession, but require that keepers obtain a permit and have microchips implanted in their animals.

Finally, be aware that it is illegal to buy or sell turtles with carapaces less than 4 inches in length in the United States, except for educational or scientific purposes. This is a particularly important consideration when breeding prolific turtles, such as snapping turtles, because you will have to care for the offspring until for at least one year, while waiting for them to attain the minimum size necessary.

Sexing Snapping Turtles

If, after considering the proposition carefully, you decide to breed snapping turtles, you will need at least one sexual pair of animals. To be sure that you have a sexed pair, you must be able to distinguish one sex from the other.

This can be a difficult task with young snapping turtles, as the differences between the two are negligible. However, by the time they reach about 6 inches in length, it becomes much easier to discern their sex.

Male snapping turtles have slightly longer tails than females do. Additionally, their vents are located in a more distal location (toward the tip of the tail) than they are in females. This vent location enables the males to reach the female's vent when attempting to mate.

Unlike most other turtles, the plastrons of male and female snapping turtles are not very different. This is due in part to the flattened shape of snapping turtle carapaces and the reduced size of their plastrons.

Pre-Breeding Conditioning

Once you have obtained a sexual pair, you must begin conditioning them for breeding. This is important because animals that are not in very good condition may not be able to handle the rigors of cycling and breeding.

Take the turtles to visit your veterinarian, who will be able to ascertain their health status. Some veterinarians may only perform a visual inspection, but others may collect biological samples for additional testing.

If your vet determines that your turtles are not healthy, take whatever steps are recommended to rectify the problem before commencing breeding trials.

Once you are certain that your turtles are in good health, it is time to initiate your breeding protocols.

Cycling

Cycling is a term used to describe the practice of providing captive reptiles with an annual variation in temperature (or other factors, such as photoperiod).

The concept seeks to mimic the natural seasonal cycle of the reptile in question. Because many reptiles from temperate habitats tend to reproduce seasonally, it stands to reason that such cycles prime their bodies for breeding. Some empirical data correlates this fact, such as the seasonal testicular growth common in some species.

In some species, proper cycling appears to be necessary for successful reproduction in captivity, while other species reproduce quite successfully with no variation in temperature or any other factor.

Snapping turtle breeders have found both approaches to be successful, although most prefer to provide a seasonal cycle to their captives. Snapping turtles from the northern reaches of their range clearly experience strong seasonal variations in the wild, but those from the tropics experience few climactic differences over the course of the year.

This wide geographic range of the species likely plays a role, making it important to consider the geographic origin of your breeding stock. Success is more likely when both of your turtles hail from the same area and you provide them with a seasonal scheme characteristic of their homeland.

You can cycle your snapping turtles in any of several ways. Some keepers with outdoor enclosures simply allow their captives to experience the natural outdoor temperatures in the area. This is a risky approach in areas with cold winters, but if the pond is at least 12 inches deeper than the level of the ice, your turtles should be able to survive the winter. In other words, if your pond freezes to a depth of 24 inches, the pond must be at least 36 inches deep, to give them a reasonable chance of remaining above freezing temperatures.

Other keepers elect to provide yearly temperature fluctuations for indoor enclosures. Some continue to provide a basking spot as per normal, but allow the water temperature to drop for two to four months, while others reduce the intensity (or duration of) the basking light along with a reduction in water temperatures. Still others turn off the lights completely during the winter while also letting the water temperature drop.

All of these strategies have proven successful, but some keepers have also had success without any type of cycling.

The takeaway from this is that several different techniques and approaches may lead to success, and so it is incumbent upon the keeper to decide what is best for their individual animals.

If you decide to subject your captives to seasonal temperature variation, reduce the amount of food offered during the "winter."

Shortly after emerging from hibernation, wild snapping turtles begin courting and mating. If you decide to subject your turtles to a seasonal cycle, breeding will usually take place shortly after raising the temperatures (and light levels, if they were lowered).

Alternatively, if you maintain constant conditions all year long, your turtles may breed at any time of year.

Pairing

Some keepers prefer to keep the sexes separate for most of the year, and only introduce them to each other during breeding trials.

One of the benefits to keeping the sexes segregated is that it often results in vigorous courting and breeding by the male. As they say, absence makes the heart grow fonder.

Additionally, maintaining turtles singly reduces the likelihood of injuries and stress for both occupants. It is also safer to feed turtles when they are kept separately.

While keeping your snapping turtles in separate enclosures is often ideal, many keepers lack the space or resources necessary to do so. Instead, most maintain breeding pairs together all year long.

While cohabitation makes it easier to house your turtles, it makes it more difficult to determine things like the date(s) of mating, which can make it difficult to predict when to expect eggs.

Those who choose to keep the sexes separately must decide whether they want to place the male in the female's cage or vice versa. Both approaches have their merits.

If you would like to mimic natural behaviors as much as possible, it makes more sense to put the female in the male's cage, as males are territorial in the wild. Generally, they maintain a well-defined home range, and will attempt to any receptive female that passes through their territory.

On the other hand, from an animal husbandry perspective, it makes more sense to move the male, as this helps reduce the amount of stress the female suffers.

Snapping turtles may begin breeding within minutes of being introduced, or they may wait for hours or days to do so. Many will wait until night falls to initiate breeding, and some may never show any interest at all.

Often, keepers of other types of reptiles respond to males with lukewarm libidos by introducing a smaller male into the enclosure. Combat often ensues, and shortly thereafter, the dominant male will often breed aggressively.

However, while separating clashing snakes, lizards or tortoises may be an easy task, stopping a fight between two large snapping turtles is an entirely different matter. In addition to placing your animals at risk of injury, you may become seriously injured in the process.

Accordingly, you should not use a subordinate male to instigate breeding behavior for snapping turtles. Instead, you must rely on husbandry adjustments (such as altering the cycling protocol or enclosure design) or changing the individuals in the breeding pair to stimulate their interest. Like humans, some turtles are simply incompatible.

Gravid

Shortly after successful copulation, suitably healthy females become gravid. Unlike many other reptiles, turtles do not offer very many signs to indicate their reproductive condition.

Manual palpation, which is a common method for determining the reproductive condition of many other reptiles, is rarely helpful with turtles. In fact, attempting to feel a female's eggs with your fingers may cause them to rupture. Accordingly, it is wise to avoid the practice entirely. Instead, the best clues lie in the female's behavior.

Many gravid snapping turtles exhibit increased appetites during the early stages of the process; however, as parturition approaches, they may cease feeding entirely.

Additionally, many gravid turtles increase the frequency with which they bask. However, snapping turtles rarely bask frequently as slider turtles and other species do, so you must watch for subtle changes in behavior. Keep in mind that snapping turtles often bask while swimming at the surface of the water, or while resting in shallow water.

Nevertheless, the only way to be certain that your turtle is gravid is by having your veterinarian perform an x-ray. This will not only verify that she is holding eggs, but it will allow you to know approximately how many eggs she is carrying.

Egg Deposition

As the time for egg deposition nears, the female will become increasingly restless. She may appear panicked, and relentlessly search for a way out of the enclosure.

At this point, the female is seeking out a place to dig a nest and deposit her eggs. Hopefully, you have designed the enclosure so that such a place is always available, but, if you have not, you must provide her with a place she finds suitable.

Typically, snapping turtles are looking for a warm area, with a particulate substrate suitable for nest construction. Wild snapping turtles use sandy beaches, muskrat lodges and riverbanks for these purposes. In captivity, a large area with a deep sand or sand-soil-mix is the most common approach.

Be aware that snapping turtles, like many other species, can be very picky about their egg deposition site. Ideally, the egg-deposition site should have a footprint of at least two to three times the size of the turtle's shell and contain substrate as deep as the turtle's shell is long.

In other words, a 12-inch female would require an egg-deposition site that provides about 2- to 3-square-feet of space and a substrate at least 12 inches deep.

If your female does not find the provided site to her liking, you will need to tweak it until she feels comfortable. This can mean loosening the substrate, compacting the substrate, providing a greater depth of substrate or moving the egg deposition site to another location in the enclosure.

This is often a challenging component of turtle breeding, and even highly experienced zookeepers occasionally have problems devising a suitable egg-laying site.

If your turtle cannot find a suitable place to lay her eggs, she may scatter the eggs in the water or retain them internally. Usually, these outcomes lead to health problems for the female, such as dystocia (egg binding).

Assuming that your turtle finds the egg deposition area suitable, she will eventually crawl into it, dig a small depression and fill it with eggs. After completing the process, she will cover the hole and reenter the water.

Although all turtles are individuals, and females may deposit their eggs during any hour of the day or night, most wild snapping turtles seem to lay their eggs during the early morning.

Female snapping turtles are often encountered during egg deposition. Photo credit: © Dcwcreations, Dreamstime.com – Snapping Turtle Eggs Photo

Egg Incubation

Keepers employ any of several different strategies for incubating snapping turtle eggs. No one method is "correct," although artificially incubating the eggs in a climate-controlled container usually leads to the greatest success.

The least labor-intensive approach is to leave the eggs where they are and let them incubate naturally. After all, snapping turtles have been incubating their eggs in just this way for millions of years.

This is most appropriate for those keeping their turtles in outdoor cages, located within the natural range of snapping turtles. However, you can also allow eggs to incubate "naturally" indoors by placing a heat lamp over the substrate containing the eggs.

Place a thermometer probe down in the egg mass (use great care to avoid damaging the eggs) to monitor the temperatures, and adjust the heat lamp until it provides appropriate temperatures for the eggs.

Snapping turtle eggs are relatively robust, and tolerate a wide range of incubation temperatures; however, temperatures between 70 and 82 degrees Fahrenheit (21 to 27 degrees Celsius) lead to the best results. Temperatures outside of this range often lead to poor hatch rates.

If you would prefer more control of the incubation process, you can excavate the egg chamber, remove the eggs and place them in a climate-controlled incubator for the remainder of their development.

Use great care when excavating the egg chamber to prevent damaging the eggs. Once you have accessed the eggs, mark the top of each with a graphite pencil. This will allow you to maintain the correct orientation when transferring the eggs to the incubator; inverting the eggs can cause the embryos to drown.

Avoid separating any eggs that have adhered to each other. While it is often possible to do so without damaging the eggs, such attempts should be left to those who have considerable experience incubating reptile eggs.

Egg Boxes

Egg boxes are small plastic storage boxes designed to hold the eggs inside the incubator. While their use is not always necessary in the strictest sense, they make it easier to maintain the climate surrounding the eggs.

Virtually any type of small plastic storage box will suffice, but consider a few things before selecting your egg boxes:

1. Be sure to select boxes that are tall enough to contain 1 or 2 inches (2.5 to 5 centimeters) of incubation media as well as the eggs, which will rest on top of the media (partially buried).
2. Whenever possible, select transparent egg boxes so that you can observe the eggs without having to open them.
3. If possible, select boxes with domed lids, which will help prevent condensation from dripping on the eggs.

You will need to make two small holes (approximately one-quarter-inch or one-half centimeter in diameter) in each box to allow for air exchange inside the egg boxes.

Some breeders prefer to monitor the temperature of the egg boxes, while others prefer to monitor the temperature of the incubator. Either method will work, although if you desire to measure the temperatures inside the egg boxes, you will need to drill additional holes to accept a temperature probe.

You can select relatively large egg boxes so that they will accommodate large clutches, or you can use relatively small egg boxes, so that you can split up the clutch into several different sub groups.

Incubation Media

Several different incubation media are appropriate for snapping turtle egg incubation. Wild snapping turtles primarily deposit their eggs in sand, which will also work in captivity. However, other substrates that work include soil, soil and sand mixtures and vermiculite. Vermiculite is one of the most common choices for incubating a wide variety of reptile eggs, as it is quite easy to attain a suitable moisture level.

The substrate not only provides a protective cushion that supports the eggs, but it also provides moisture which will keep the relative humidity of the egg box high. This will prevent the eggs from desiccating.

Too much humidity or dampness, however, can have a negative effect on the eggs, so it is important to keep enough water in the egg boxes, but not too much.

Many keepers strive to maintain humidity levels of 80 percent in the egg chamber, but others simply watch the eggs and adjust the humidity accordingly. If the eggs begin to exhibit wrinkles, they are drying out and more water is necessary. Conversely, if they begin to swell or exude fluid, the humidity should be lowered.

Some authorities recommend specific ratios of water and vermiculite, but as vermiculite absorbs water from the air, it is impossible to know how saturated the vermiculite was when you started.

Accordingly, the best approach is to judge the moisture with your hands. Beginning with dry vermiculite, slowly add water while stirring the mixture. The goal is to dampen the vermiculite just enough that it clumps when compressed in your hand. However, if water drips from the media when you squeeze it, the vermiculite is too damp.

The Incubator

You can either purchase a commercially produced incubator or construct your own. However, most beginning breeders are better served by purchasing a commercial incubator than making their own.

Commercial Incubators

Commercial egg incubators come in myriad styles and sizes. Some of the most popular models are similar to those used to incubate poultry eggs (these are often available for purchase from livestock supply retailers).

These incubators are constructed from a large foam box, fitted with a heating element and thermostat. Some models feature a fan for circulating air; while helpful for maintaining a uniform thermal environment, models that lack these fans are acceptable.

You can place an incubation medium directly in the bottom of these types of incubators, although it is preferable to place the media (and eggs) inside small plastic storage boxes, which are then placed inside the incubator.

These incubators are usually affordable and easy to use, although their foam-based construction makes them less durable than most premium incubators are.

Other incubators are constructed from metal or plastic boxes; feature a clear door, an enclosed heating element and a thermostat. Some units also feature a backup thermostat, which can provide some additional protection in case the primary thermostat fails.

These types of incubators usually outperform economy, foam-based models, but they also bear higher price tags. Either style will work, but, if you plan to breed turtles for many years, premium models usually present the best option.

Homemade Incubators

Although incubators can be constructed in a variety of ways, using many different materials and designs, two basic designs are most common.

The first type of homemade incubator consists of a plastic, glass or wood box, and a simple heat source, such as a piece of heat tape or a low-wattage heat lamp. The heating source must be attached to a thermostat to keep the temperatures consistent. A thermometer is also necessary for monitoring the temperatures of the incubator.

Some keepers make these types of incubators from wood, while others prefer plastic or foam. Although glass is a poor insulator, aquariums often serve as acceptable incubators; however, you must purchase or construct a solid top to retain heat.

Place a brick on the bottom of the incubator, and place the egg box on top of the brick, so that the eggs are not resting directly on the heat tape. The brick will also provide thermal mass to the incubator, which will help maintain a more consistent temperature.

The other popular incubator design adds a quantity of water to the design to help maintain consistent temperatures and a higher humidity. To build such a unit, begin with an aquarium fitted with a glass or plastic lid.

Place a brick in the bottom of the aquarium and add about two gallons of water to the aquarium; ideally, the water level should stop right below the top of the brick.

Add an aquarium heater to the water and set the thermostat to the desired temperature. Place the egg box on the brick, insert a temperature probe into the egg box and cover the aquarium with the lid (you may need to purchase a lid designed to allow the cords to pass through it).

This type of incubator works by heating the water, which will in turn heat the air inside the incubator, which will heat the eggs. Although it can take several days of repeated adjustments to get these types of incubators set to the exact temperature you would like, they are very stable once established.

Incubation Temperature and Duration

As with the adult animals, the biological processes taking place inside reptile eggs are determined by the temperature at which they are kept. The warmer the environment is, the quicker the eggs develop; the cooler the environment is, the longer it takes the eggs to complete their development.

This basic principle holds true for snapping turtles. (Yntema, 1978) However, this does not mean that their eggs can be incubated at any temperature. Eggs kept below the minimum acceptable temperature will fail to live, just as those kept above the maximum acceptable temperature.

In fact, this leads to the death of some percentage of snapping turtles in the wild. For example, if a snapping turtle deposits her eggs in a shaded area, they are unlikely to remain warm enough to develop properly.

The ideal range for snapping turtle egg incubation ranges from the high 70s Fahrenheit to the low 80s Fahrenheit. Higher incubation temperatures cause the embryos to develop more quickly than those incubated at lower temperatures do.

These are relatively low temperatures relative to other reptiles, and – depending on the temperature of your home – you may be able to incubate the eggs at "room temperature."

However, doing so will invariably expose the eggs to temperature fluctuations. Minor temperature fluctuations are not harmful to the eggs, but massive swings in temperature predispose the eggs to failure or cause the young to be abnormal.

The duration of incubation varies depending on the temperature and the length of the female's gestation period. Most snapping turtle eggs hatch approximately 60 to 90 days after being deposited.

Sex Determination

The sex of snapping turtles is determined by the temperature at which they are incubated. This phenomenon is called temperature dependent sex determination (abbreviated TDS or TDSD) and is common among many different reptile lineages, including crocodilians, geckos and many other chelonians.

Accordingly, if you can control the temperature of the egg mass (or individual eggs) with precision, you can deliberately create male or female hatchlings.

Reptiles exhibit two different forms of TSD:

1. Type I TSD describes animals that become male when incubated above a given threshold temperature.
2. Type II TSD describes animals that become male only when incubated between two different temperature thresholds; eggs incubated above or below this intermediate range become female.

Snapping turtles exhibit Type II TSD. (Justin R. St. Juliana, 2004)

Temperatures between about 70.7 degrees Fahrenheit (21.5 degrees Celsius) and 81.6 degrees Fahrenheit (27.6 degrees Celsius) produce male hatchlings, while temperatures below 70.7 or above 81.6 produce females. Temperatures near each of these threshold temperatures result in clutches containing both sexes.

However, eggs incubated at the lower end of this range frequently fail to develop properly, so the primary threshold temperature relevant to snapping turtle egg incubation is 81.6 degrees.

In practice, most snapping turtle breeders incubate their eggs at temperatures of about 80 degrees. When trying to produce females (or a mix of both sexes) they increase the temperature by a couple of degrees.

Neonatal Husbandry

Remove the turtles from the incubator as they hatch. Use a gentle touch with the delicate creatures and move them to the nursery container.

A hatchling snapping turtle photographed next to a U.S. quarter to provide a sense of scale.

The nursery container should be constructed from a small plastic storage box (you can split the clutch among several different boxes to reduce the stress on the hatchlings). Drill or melt a few small ventilation holes in the top and place a few layers of paper towels on the bottom.

Add a very shallow water dish to the center of the cage (a 3-inch plant saucer works well) and keep it full of clean water. Leave the hatchlings inside the nursery for at least 24 hours to ensure they have absorbed their egg yolks are have become active. Any with egg yolks that still protrude from their plastron should be left in the nursery. Never attempt to remove the egg yolk – just be patient and wait for it to shrivel and fall off.

Once a turtle has become active, you can move it to its "permanent" home. You can house a few hatchlings together in the same habitat, but avoid overcrowding them, which can lead to squabbles and injuries. Be sure there are more places to hide than there are turtles in the tank.

You can begin feeding them almost immediately after placing them in their new homes, but many will not begin feeding for a few days.

Chapter 11: Unusual Snapping Turtles

Snapping turtles are highly variable animals; different individuals from the same pond (or even the same clutch) often exhibit slightly different colors. This is largely due to individual variation, but every once in a while, a genetic mutation pops up that gives rise to animals whose unusual looks far surpass what can be explained by normal individual variation.

For example, instead of being clad in browns, grays and greens, some snapping turtles hatch as white, pink or yellow animals. Often these individuals are quite striking, and snapping turtle enthusiasts prize them.

These types of genetic mutations are relatively rare. Some researchers contend that amelanism – one of the most common color mutations – occurs in approximately one snapping turtle out of every 30,000.

Such color mutations are extremely rare among animals that rely on camouflage to survive. Conspicuous in their natural habitats, these boldly colored animals often fall victim to predators before reaching their first birthday. While those few who survive to adulthood are likely safe from most predators, their bright colors still serve as a disadvantage when trying to ambush prey.

Captive specimens, by contrast, need not hide from predators and have food provided to them, so their strange colors do not represent a hindrance to survival. Indeed, these fancifully colored individuals often benefit from more attention from their keepers than their normal-appearing counterparts receive.

Nevertheless, because of the way in which these mutations are passed from parent to offspring, these spectacular animals remain relatively rare, even among captive populations. Yet strangely, this same mechanism helps to ensure the perpetuation of the mutant gene.

Common Mutations

In contrast to some other common reptile pets, such as ball pythons (*Python regius*) and leopard geckos (*Eublepharis macularius*), for which many color mutations have been discovered, only a handful of color mutations have been discovered occurring in snapping turtles.

New mutations do appear from time to time, but sometimes, the distinction between mutations and individual variation is difficult to determine. Additionally, breeding trials are necessary to determine whether the trait is the result of random, individual variation, or if it represents a heritable condition.

At the time of this publication, three types of color mutations – amelanism, hypomelanism and leucism -- are well represented in the captive gene pool.

Amelanism

Amelanism is a condition that prevents animals from producing the pigment melanin. Without this pigment, the animals appear lighter than they normally would. Such animals are often called "albino."

However, amelanistic snapping turtles are rarely pure white; they usually have yellow or pink hues as well. Like most other amelanistic animals, amelanistic snapping turtles have bright red or pink eyes. This occurs because without melanin, the blood vessels in the eyes are visible.

As with typical snapping turtles, amelanistic snapping turtles often harbor a thin coat of algae. However, because of the light coloration of the animals, the green growth on their shells often presents an interesting visual contrast.

Amelanism is inherited in simple recessive fashion, which means that individuals have to have two copies of the mutant gene to display the trait. Animals with one copy of the amelanistic gene and one copy of the "wild type" gene look normal. However, these "carriers" are able to produce amelanistic offspring, if their breeding partner also has at least one copy of the mutant gene (see "Patterns of Inheritance" for further discussion).

Note the red eyes and green coat of algae on this amelanistic snapping turtle.

Hypomelanism

Hypomelanism is a genetic mutation that causes animals to produce less melanin than normal. Unlike amelanistic individuals, whose complete lack of melanin yields pale yellow skin, hypomelanistic animals usually look orange or rich yellow.

There are several different forms of hypomelanism and much remains to be learned about hypomelanistic traits in snapping turtles. Some forms of hypomelanism are inherited in recessive fashion, while others are caused by incompletely dominant genes.

Some forms of the condition are compatible with other forms in other common pet species; it remains to be seen if the same proves true of hypomelanistic snapping turtles.

Leucism

Neither the terms "leucism" nor "leucistic" appear in many dictionaries. These terms are often applied to animals with a characteristic color scheme, in which they exhibit white skin and dark eyes. However, the veterinary definition of the term has more to do with the method of color disruption, rather than the overall appearance of the animal. Nevertheless, it is used relatively consistently among most animal keepers.

Leucistic snapping turtles, however, do not fit this definition perfectly. While snapping turtles have white skin and dark eyes, as most other leucistic animals do, their shells are generally light brown in color.

Whether or not such turtles should be called leucistic, they are gorgeous animals, and many keepers find them quite beautiful.

Patterns of Inheritance

Snapping turtles inherit genetically based mutations in one of several characteristic patterns.

Turtles receive one copy of each gene from their mother and one from their father. Some genes affect the animal's appearance when only one copy is present, while others require two copies of a gene to express the associated trait.

Animals with two copies of the same gene are said to be homozygous. Conversely, animals with one copy of a mutant gene and one copy of the normal gene are called heterozygous.

Simple Recessive
Simple recessive traits are only expressed when an animal has two copies of the mutant gene. However, normal looking, but heterozygous animals may produce offspring that display the trait associated with the gene, if the other parent has a copy of the gene as well.

Dominant
Dominant traits are expressed whenever they are present, regardless of the other gene in the pair. Accordingly, dominant traits become very common in a given gene pool. For example, the genes associated with the normal appearance of snapping turtles are dominant over most genes.

There is no visual difference between an animal with one copy of a dominant gene or two copies of the gene. However, animals that are homozygous for the dominant trait only produce young that express the dominant gene.

Incompletely Dominant

Incompletely dominant mutations are similar to dominant mutations except that those with one copy of the gene look different from those with two copies of the mutant gene.

Often, heterozygous animals display a trait (such as some forms of hypomelanism), while homozygous animals display a more extreme version of the trait (such as the so-called "super hypomelanistic" animals).

Often, incompletely dominant mutations are called co-dominant mutations. However, this terminology is not technically correct, as animals that display co-dominant traits possess more than one mutant gene.

Polygenetic Traits

Some physical traits of snapping turtles are determined by the complicated interactions of several different genes. Size potential and growth rate, for example, are likely controlled by a collection of genes.

Polygenetic traits are not inherited in a predictable fashion. However, they can often be refined through selective breeding efforts.

Genetic Traits and Marketing

Unusual specimens often command very high prices, which can make turtle breeding a profitable endeavor in some cases. While there is nothing inherently wrong with this fact, the prospect of high profits often leads keepers to experience problems.

While some of these problems are born of honest mistakes or misunderstandings, others are the result of outright fraud.

For example, unusually colored snapping turtles hatch all the time. However, as the vast majority of these animals look unusual due to normal variation, these traits are rarely reproducible.

Accordingly, those who hatch unusual looking turtles should attempt to reproduce the mutation before labelling it as a genetically inheritable condition. However, in an effort to get the animals to market quickly, some breeders market the animals in deceptive ways.

Accordingly, it is always wise to do your homework before deciding to purchase a snapping turtle with a rare color mutation. Additionally, it is wise to avoid purchasing turtles from shady, disreputable or evasive breeders, particularly if they are making extraordinary claims about their animals.

Chapter 12: Supplemental Information

Never stop learning more about your new pet's natural history, biology and captive care. Doing so will help you provide your new pet with the highest quality of life possible.

Further Reading

Bookstores and online book retailers often offer a treasure trove of information that will advance your quest for knowledge. While books represent an additional cost involved in reptile care, you can consider it an investment in your pet's well-being. Your local library may also carry some books about turtles, which you can borrow for no charge.

University libraries are a great place for finding old, obscure or academically oriented books about turtles. You may not be allowed to borrow these books if you are not a student, but you can view and read them at the library.

Herpetology: An Introductory Biology of Amphibians and Reptiles

By Laurie J. Vitt, Janalee P. Caldwell

Academic Press, 2013

Understanding Reptile Parasites: A Basic Manual for Herpetoculturists & Veterinarians

By Roger Klingenberg D.V.M.

Advanced Vivarium Systems, 1997

Infectious Diseases and Pathology of Reptiles: Color Atlas and Text

Elliott Jacobson

CRC Press

Designer Reptiles and Amphibians

Richard D. Bartlett, Patricia Bartlett

Barron's Educational Series

Magazines

Like books, magazines can offer an abundance of information. Additionally, because they are typically published several times each year, they often provide more current information than books do.

Reptiles Magazine

www.reptilesmagazine.com/

This publication covers all facets of reptile husbandry, breeding and care.

Practical Reptile Keeping

http://www.practicalreptilekeeping.co.uk/

Practical Reptile Keeping is a popular publication aimed at beginning and advanced hobbies. Topics include the care and maintenance of popular reptiles as well as information on wild reptiles.

Websites

With the explosion of the internet, it is easier to find information about reptiles than it has ever been. However, this growth has cause an increase in the proliferation of both good information and bad information.

While knowledgeable breeders, keepers and academics operate some websites, other webmasters lack the same dedication and scientific rigor. Anyone with a computer and internet connection can launch a website and say virtually anything they want about turtles. Accordingly, as with all other research, consider the source of the information before making any husbandry decisions.

The Reptile Report

www.thereptilereport.com/

The Reptile Report is a news-aggregating website that accumulates interesting stories and features about reptiles from around the world.

Kingsnake.com

www.kingsnake.com

Started as a small website for gray-banded kingsnake enthusiasts, Kingsnake.com has become one of the largest reptile-oriented portals in the hobby. Includes classifieds, breeder directories, message forums and other resources.

The Vivarium and Aquarium News

www.vivariumnews.com/

The online version of the former publication, The Vivarium and Aquarium News provides in-depth coverage of different reptiles and amphibians in a captive and wild context.

Journals

Journals are the primary place professional scientists turn when they need to learn about turtles. While they may not make light reading, hobbyists stand to learn a great deal from journals.

Herpetologica

www.hljournals.org/

Published by The Herpetologists' League, Herpetologica, and its companion publication, Herpetological Monographs cover all aspects of reptile and amphibian research.

Journal of Herpetology

www.ssarherps.org/

Produced by the Society for the Study of Reptiles and Amphibians, the Journal of Herpetology is a peer-reviewed publication covering a variety of reptile-related topics.

Copeia

www.asihcopeiaonline.org/

Copeia is published by the American Society of Ichthyologists and Herpetologists. A peer-reviewed journal, Copeia covers all aspects of the biology of reptiles, amphibians and fish.

Nature

www.nature.com/

Although Nature covers all aspects of the natural world, there is plenty to appeal to turtle enthusiasts.

Supplies

While you can obtain some of the supplies you need from local pet stores, home improvement stores and grocery stores, you may need to search widely to find some supplies and tools. Some of the following retailers sell a variety of husbandry tools and supplies.

Big Apple Pet Supply

http://www.bigappleherp.com

Big Apple Pet Supply carries most common husbandry equipment, including heating devices, water dishes and substrates.

LLLReptile

http://www.lllreptile.com

LLL Reptile carries a wide variety of husbandry tools, heating devices, lighting products and more.

Doctors Foster and Smith

http://www.drsfostersmith.com

Foster and Smith is a veterinarian-owned retailer that supplies husbandry-related items to pet keepers.

Support Organizations

Sometimes, the best way to learn about tortoises is to reach out to other keepers and breeders. Check out these organizations, and search for others in your geographic area.

The National Reptile & Amphibian Advisory Council

http://www.nraac.org/

The National Reptile & Amphibian Advisory Council seeks to educate the hobbyists, legislators and the public about reptile and amphibian related issues.

American Veterinary Medical Association

www.avma.org

The AVMA is a good place for Americans to turn if you are having trouble finding a suitable reptile veterinarian.

The World Veterinary Association

http://www.worldvet.org/

The World Veterinary Association is a good resource for finding suitable reptile veterinarians worldwide.

Index

Achilles tendonitis, 132
Anatomy, 22
Behavioral Patterns, 30
Bleach, 76
Breeding, 32, 98, 100
cage, 46
camouflage, 21
circulatory, 23
Color, 16
Costs, 45
Defensive Strategies, 31
Ecology, 39
eggs, 9, 25, 26, 33, 41, 52, 83, 91, 96, 98, 103, 104, 105, 106, 107, 108, 109, 110, 111, 112, 113, 114, 115
Enclosure, 48
eyes, 21, 70, 82, 119, 120
Gender, 79
Geography, 39
Growth, 26
growth ring, 19
Heat, 45, 59, 60, 61, 62
Heat Cables, 62
Heat Tape, 61
husbandry, 126, 128
Husbandry, 116

Intelligence, 29
keels, 19
Lifespan, 28
locomotion, 20
Maintenance, 76
Metabolism, 29
Morphology, 16
Myths, 46
online, 124
parasites, 13, 42, 94, 95
Phylogeny, 34
Prey, 40
pulmonary, 23
Records, 78
Reproductive, 24
Rheostats, 63
scales, 19
scutes, 17
Shedding, 27
shell, 22
Size, 17, 53, 122
skull, 22
Taxonomy, 34
Thermostats, 63
veterinarian, 128, 129
water change, 77
Water Quality, 73

References

Anderson, S. P. (2003). The Phylogenetic Definition of Reptilia. *Systematic Biology*.

Crawford, N. G. (2012). A phylogenomic analysis of turtles. *Molecular Phylogenetics and Evolution*.

Feuer, R. C. (1971). Intergradation of the Snapping Turtles Chelydra serpentina serpentina (Linnaeus, 1758) and Chelydra serpentina osceola Stejneger, 1918. *Herpetologica*.

Justin R. St. Juliana, R. M. (2004). The impact of behavioral and physiological maternal effects on offspring sex ratio in the common snapping turtle, Chelydra serpentina. *Behavioral Ecology and Sociobiology*.

Yntema, C. L. (1978). Incubation Times for Eggs of the Turtle Chelydra serpentina (Testudines: Chelydridae) at Various Temperatures. *Herpetologica*.

Published by IMB Publishing 2015

Copyright and Trademarks: This publication is Copyrighted 2015 by IMB Publishing. All products, publications, software and services mentioned and recommended in this publication are protected by trademarks. In such instance, all trademarks & copyright belong to the respective owners. All rights reserved. No part of this book may be reproduced or transferred in any form or by any means, graphic, electronic, or mechanical, including photocopying, recording, taping, or by any information storage retrieval system, without the written permission of the authors. Pictures used in this book are either royalty free pictures bought from stock-photo websites or have the source mentioned underneath the picture.

Disclaimer and Legal Notice: This product is not legal or medical advice and should not be interpreted in that manner. You need to do your own due-diligence to determine if the content of this product is right for you. The author and the affiliates of this product are not liable for any damages or losses associated with the content in this product. While every attempt has been made to verify the information shared in this publication, neither the author nor the affiliates assume any responsibility for errors, omissions or contrary interpretation of the subject matter herein. Any perceived slights to any specific person(s) or organization(s) are purely unintentional. We have no control over the nature, content and availability of the web sites listed in this book. The inclusion of any web site links does not necessarily imply a recommendation or endorse the views expressed within them. IMB Publishing takes no responsibility for, and will not be liable for, the websites being temporarily unavailable or being removed from the Internet. The accuracy and completeness of information provided herein and opinions stated herein are not guaranteed or warranted to produce any particular results, and the advice and strategies, contained herein may not be suitable for every individual. The author shall not be liable for any loss incurred as a consequence of the use and application, directly or indirectly, of any information presented in this work. This publication is designed to provide information in regards to the subject matter covered. The information included in this book has been compiled to give an overview of the subject s and detail some of the symptoms, treatments etc. that are available to people with this condition. It is not intended to give medical advice. For a firm diagnosis of your condition, and for a treatment plan suitable for you, you should consult your doctor or consultant. The writer of this book and the publisher are not responsible for any damages or negative consequences following any of the treatments or methods highlighted in this book. Website links are for informational purposes and should not be seen as a personal endorsement; the same applies to the products detailed in this book. The reader should also be aware that although the web links included were correct at the time of writing, they may become out of date in the future.

www.ingramcontent.com/pod-product-compliance
Lightning Source LLC
Chambersburg PA
CBHW070502100426
42743CB00010B/1734